STAR POWER:
Internet Celebrity

"The only resource you will ever need to reach Millions of excited customers instantly!"

Star Power: Internet Celebrity the successful guide to Advertising and Marketing on the Internet to the entertainment industry is an absolute best seller resource and a must read book for anyone who presently has an online business, organization or is contemplating one. Sonya Swinton brings her 10 years of experience in advertising & marketing management and her savvy expertise on Internet e-commerce together in one book that offers the novice as well as the experienced business professional a jump start education on doing business on the Internet with the media moguls in the exciting world of entertainment.

STAR POWER:
Internet Celebrity

Successful Advertising, Marketing and Promoting to the Entertainment Industry on the Internet

SONYA DEVONNE SWINTON

Writers Club Press

San Jose New York Lincoln Shanghai

STAR POWER: Internet Celebrity
Successful Advertising, Marketing and Promoting to the
Entertainment Industry on the Internet

Writers Club Press
an imprint of iUniverse, Inc.

For information address:
iUniverse, Inc.
5220 S. 16th St., Suite 200
Lincoln, NE 68512
www.iuniverse.com

Cover Designed By Swinton International Enterprises

ISBN: 0-595-22164-5

Printed in the United States of America

Dedication

This book is dedicated to all of the present and future individuals and organizations that are pursuing or would like to pursue the world of entertainment as a career or vocation and need assistance on the Internet with their advertising, marketing and promotion strategies.

A special dedication to my parents Billy C. & Lonetta, my brothers Darrell and Keith, brother-in-law Derek, my oldest sister Scharyl, and my three nieces Shauntae, Allison and Chutney.

Contents

Acknowledgements

A big thank you to the many people that have contributed to this book. I dearly appreciate the advice of the professional team of staff, associates and volunteers of Swinton International Enterprises, Community TV USA Network and the Royal Swinton Society. My heart felt appreciation and admiration to author and relative, Eddie Faye Gates. Mrs. Gates professional guidance & warm encouragement and editing skills have contributed to this work tremendously. A special thanks to my friend Tara (Hamilton) Weeks, author and aunt Gwendolyn Swinton and cousin Dedra Swinton Arthur for their editing and technical advice and expertise. I thank my family and friends for all of their support.

I appreciate the wonderful and talented people that I have met in the following entertainment and multi-media organizations:

Patricia Spurlock and Sandy Pastoor, the American Women in Radio and TV; Paul Barry, National Academy of Television Arts and Sciences; Daryl P. Friedman and Heidi Gerber, National Academy of Recording Arts and Sciences' MusiCare, the American Film Institute's Los Angeles International Film Festival; Roger Carter, the Royal TV Society; John Mason, the Society of Motion Picture & Television Engineers, the Royal Photographic Society members, and the British Academy of Film and Television staff.

A special thank you to my friend and photographer, Avonda Smith for the cover photo. Last but definitely not least, I would like to thank Jerry Gallun, Robert Butler and my cousins, Yolanda Swinton Newton and Maurice Swinton for rescuing my brand new ailing computer from my experimentation of creativity with his computer expertise and words of encouragement (*"Sonya, you need to stick to writing and leave the computer programming to me".*) I most definitely agree with that antidote with a happy resolve. And most of all, I would like to acknowledge God the Almighty for blessing & surrounding me with a marvelous group of successful and resourceful people.

Moreover, the writing of this book was an educational, enlightening and humbling experience that I truly enjoyed the journey. Furthermore, thank you the reader for allowing me to share this time with you. I sincerely hope that you will be encouraged and inspired to build a superstar website on the Internet that will be able to sale, market and promote your best professional services and products to the exciting world of entertainment, multi-media and interactive production companies and individuals.

Introduction

How a little obscured agency named Community TV USA Network went from a zero on line presence, to a chart topping success of being rated in the top five percent of all the major search engines, rivaling major corporate mass media and commercial TV stations in just three short months.

My Story-

"We all vote for Sonya Swinton to lead our online advertising and marketing website campaign." All in favor say, yes! *"Did I hear my name called"*, as I walked into the crowded boardroom? Opps! Someone forgot to inform Ms. Swinton of her extra duties. Has this ever happened to you? Have you ever been heaved up the creek without a paddle or should I say without a marketing budget for online e-commerce endeavors? On a Thursday at 3:30 pm three years ago, I was informed that our Community TV USA Network website was finally going on line the next week and we needed a brilliant marketing plan, ASAP. I had absolutely zero budgets to start. My only compensation would be the commissions from our banner advertisement and link exchange programs.

After the initial shock, I gathered my composer and decided to take on the challenge. So what if we were short on cash, I knew of some talented professionals that were long on creativity and imagination and would be eager to display their work for a piece of the action. As a professional photographer, I decided to use our large supply files of community photos to grab our site visitors' attention. We decided to use the former *zing.com* (it shutdown on July 2, 2001) compression tool for our photo pages.

In a short period of time, we had an international audience knocking at our door. We began to consistently get site visits from all over the world, including the United Kingdom, Japan, Australia, and even Indonesia. Wow! They seemed to have been drawn by our display of local community pictures. A couple of months later, I received an urgent phone call from our elated public relations department manager. As he screamed, "we did it"! We made the top ten sites visited in all of the major search engines. We begin pulling up Alta Vista, Yahoo, Excite, Hotbot, GoTo, Lycros and AOL search engines to see our website's placement. Sure enough, Community TV USA Network *ctvnusa.com* was second to *ABC.com* in one of the popular search engines and rated number one in the other major search engines.

Hooray! Okay, now what? Back to reality…

"Where do we go from here?" everyone shrugged. We have found that getting on top is easy, but staying on top is the kicker. If you would like your unknown website to become the *top of the line* and *talk of the town* in a short period of time, then read on.

STAR POWER:

Internet Celebrity

Successful Advertising & Marketing
To the Entertainment Industry
On the Internet

Chapter 1

What is an Internet Celebrity?

Introducing the Cyberspace Celebrity Queen:

SONYA D. SWINTON

Move over Liz Taylor, step back Oprah Winfrey, and eat your heart out Britany Spears—from the film, television and music star personalities, introducing Sonya D! She has it *all* covered without a sweat. *"Some of us are born to be celebrities—or in my case, just born to look like one"*.

Introducing the ultimate international cyberspace celebrity, SONYA D. SWINTON! It's not what you know or who you know, but…Who knows you? Introducing the original Internet celebrity, Sonya D! Jeremy Alexander, public affairs officer of Community TV USA Network states with enthusiasm that Sonya Swinton is one of the firsts to coin the term *Internet Celebrity*. As an Internet pioneer, she has become a master at digital technology advertising and marketing on line. Star Power: Internet Celebrity is sure to enlighten the masses on the creative potential of this new technology.

I am originally the first *Internet Celebrity* you will ever meet that will honestly admit to it. Who am I, you ask? I am Sonya D! (my stage name) the ultimate *"Cyberspace Celebrity Queen for a Lifetime"*. I have discovered the phenomenon power of cyberspace can make anyone an *international cyberstar* without much effort. I like that, because I hate to sweat. I'm just kidding; I enjoy my fitness workouts as much as anyone else does. I am probably one of the very first to coin the term Internet celebrity. Internet celebrity status is for those individuals who are *initially* made famous by mass exposure on the World Wide Web. Come with me as I introduce to you the Star Power of the Internet *"where fame and stardom is only a galaxy away"*. Check out the website at: *www. internet-celebrity.com.*

Childhood Dreams

My foundation for becoming an *Internet celebrity* started as a dream far back in my childhood. The lovely author, Mrs. Eddie Faye Gates states in her precious family book, *Miz Lucy's Cookies: And Other Links in my Black Family Support System* that, *"if I could turn back the clock and pluck a thing from the past to give to today's children, it would be a loving family like mine, and the loving extension to that family"*. I agree with her sentiments because my loving family and friends also were what kept me going through the challenging times as well as through the rewarding times in my childhood. In her second book, *They Came Searching: How Blacks Sought The Promise Land in Tulsa*, Mrs. Gates continues with her strong endorsement of black families. She credits the strong black family unit for being the cause of the survival of blacks in Oklahoma, especially those in Tulsa who endured and survived the worst race riot in U.S. history, The Tulsa Race Riot of 1921! *www.tulsa-riot.com.*

My childhood played out like an adventurous *odyssey*. Except for a few scraped knees, bee stings and mosquito bites, I lived through childhood without one broken bone. That is a great feat considering I use to swing like a *monkey* on my backyard swing set and jungle gym. How did I become so content with being by myself? You can blame my sophisticated degree of self-assurance on my parents. I make no apologies for my high self-confidence and high self-esteem because my parents taught me to respect authority with moral integrity and ethical character but stay far away from foolish people. Therefore, I have never been one of those people who just blindly followed the foolish crowd because a *fool* said so. My parents and grandparents used to tell me to stay away from people with *shady* moral character; whether they are rich or poor is not important. The most important virtues to look for in an individual are integrity, trustfulness and a keen sense of justice. These characteristics should never be compromised and are *royally* priceless.

Speaking of royalty, one day, when I was six years old, I ran home from school and I told my dad when he got home from work that the kids had been teasing me because my two front teeth happened to have been missing at the time. As a diva-in-training, I didn't think that "Snaggle Tooth" was a funny nickname for me. My dad told me that they were only teasing and not to worry because in his eyes *"I was a princess."* After the pep talk, I assumed that I was a "princess" and I went back to school the next day and let everybody know that I was royalty. Consequently, my feelings of royalty never wore off and I decided right then that I would wear that title for a *lifetime*. I ran for the campus queen of my university, and I won. Although, having the world revolve around me was quite an interesting experience in royalty protocol, I mostly enjoy volunteering my time to worthwhile causes for those less fortunate.

How did I become an INTERNET CELEBRITY? Well instantly, of course. My parents always said that I was a star, but they just didn't know what galaxy. Thank goodness for the World Wide Web. However, my instant celebrity status comes with setbacks as well as perks. Unlike the TV and movie superstars who are mostly known for their fame and fortune, I am ultimately famous and my fortune is on its way. So you see, I can shop at the upscale shopping centers, and get all the last minute bargains without flack from store clerks trying to make high-pressure sales and causing me to overspend. I can also bypass the stares of people in line wondering if I am ever going to outgrow my flamboyant attitude for the ordinary person's taste for bargains. And the answer is…apparently not because I do not have a need to.

For instance, a nationally known celebrity with tremendous admiration and recognition would need a bodyguard, *"wouldn't she"*? But in my case, I thoroughly enjoy being incognito when I want to be. Just because I am ordinary doesn't mean that I have to *look* or *act* ordinary. Who made it a law that us average, run-of-the-mill folks can't stretch our imaginations beyond a shoestring budget? With my vast imagination, the stars and the moon are not the limit. This resource book was intended to be an information tool to assist you in your advertising, marketing & promotion campaign, and to introduce you to the Internet Celebrity and Royal Swinton Society websites.

This book was also written for busy individuals on the go and for not-so-busy individuals who have trouble absorbing quite a bite of detailed information, like me. Writing about advertising and marketing is what I know best, and becoming a celebrity is more my forte. I feel that having *celebrity appeal* is a very important key to becoming an Internet celebrity.

Celebrity Appeal

A colleague of mine told me that several times she had attended entertainment award dinners during which even well known celebrities had come up to her and told her that she *looked* like a celebrity. She said that she didn't have any problem in getting respect from wealthy celebrities when she asked them if she could pose for pictures with them. In fact, she said that she gets more flack from her average everyday co-workers than she has ever gotten from multi-millionaire celebrities. Hmm, sounds like she is in the wrong business. I encouraged her to become an Internet Celebrity and let her star-quality looks grace the World Wide Web; then everyone else could also be able to admire her star potential. Because of her shyness, she said that she didn't think she had the right look. I responded to her that it wasn't so much the right look but the right self-confident attitude that makes a true star. I asked her if she ever noticed that real celebrities are not necessarily the most beautiful, handsome, talented or smartest; although they can role-play characters with that quality.

Say to yourself, *"I can be an internet celebrity, too!"* It won't be long before this age of the superhighway's Internet becomes the ultimate vehicle for ideas, products and services being quickly advertised, marketed and promoted worldwide. Ordinary looking people are the stars of today as well as tomorrow. For instance, one day I was searching the Internet and I kept coming up with the same banner advertisement of an ordinary looking teenager on America Online (AOL) in an advertisement on classmates' connections. That got me to pondering the idea that anyone could have been in that advertisement. I feel that ordinary looking people are needed on the Internet advertisements just as well as their glamorous counterparts. It is said that ordinary looking people are needed by advertisers on commercials in order to convey believability to the masses.

Take for instance, one day a casting agent was recruiting for a healthcare commercial and she asked an oriental coworker of mine if he would mind being cast for a healthcare commercial. The agent said that she needed an ordinary looking person, nothing glamorous. He said no, he wasn't interested, but she was persistent and hounded him into an audition for a non-speaking part. She completely ignored my handsome athletic-looking friend. Although he tried to get her attention by clearing his throat, she ignored him. Somewhat annoyed, he just came out and asked, if he could participate in the commercial. Her reply floored all of us. She told him that although she was casting for a minority part where the person could be of any gender or ethnicity, they were not casting attractive people like him and besides his skin tone was too light to be cast as an African America person. She emphasized that the 30-second commercial must automatically present each individual as a distinct culturally diverse person. *"What a bummer,"* he said exasperated, at his first opportunity to be cast in a national commercial. She advised him that commercial advertisers are subjective when it comes to selecting models in both print and television advertising.

A similar incident happened to me when I was invited by a production coordinator to participate as part of a TV studio audience. Everyone was greeted by the production assistant and given a release form to fill out; everyone except me. The production assistant immediately walked passed me. It was so obvious that a gentleman seated at the table beside me raised his hand to get the production assistant's attention for my release form. Embarrassed, she politely came over to me. She exclaimed to me that she thought that I was the announcer for that particular production and that my agent had my paperwork. (I guess that I looked somewhat overdressed for an audience member because the original announcer gave me a second look as though he had worn the wrong attire). Moral of the story, some people just look like celebrities' whether they open their mouths or not.

Entering the Entertainment Industry

I started my career in the entertainment industry by forming a performing arts group called the Military Entertainment Association while living in Okinawa, Japan. I auditioned actors, dancers, models and singers from the military personnel and their families on eight American military service bases. *My goodness, I have to say that the military community had some very talented and colorful individuals to select from.* I auditioned adults, teenagers as well as children. Our entertainment committee decided to produce a teen beauty pageant so we advertised on the military television station Far East Network (FEN), the only American station on the island. To our surprise, Americans were not the only ones watching the TV announcements; the Japanese business community was also watching.

One day while we were practicing for the pageant at the USO, some Japanese from the Okinawa Business Association approached us with their interpreters to inquire about becoming sponsors for our pageant. They not only wanted to provide the winners with gifts but they also volunteered to provide the entertainment acts during the intermission. At the pageant, the Japanese patrons purchased all of our remaining tickets. They also invited their mayor and his entourage to present the awards and key to the city to the winners. I guess they knew that the exchange of good will would bring both the United States military community and the Japanese citizens a major dose of positive publicity.

The Japanese businessmen also brought their professional performing arts school to entertain the audience even though we had not solicited their assistance. In other words, believe it are not when people want to participate, hell or high water will not stop them, and if people do not want to participate begging them to do so is a waste of time. I am comfortable with audiences from two or several thousand; it doesn't matter to me now but when I was a kid I was panic stricken like most people. My hunch is that there is really not a set way to enter the entertainment industry. When I returned to the United States from overseas, I joined my other professional colleagues in volunteering to serve on several local entertainment foundation committees. I have come to really admire and appreciate the wonderful and talented individuals that I have met through the following organizations: American Women in Radio and TV; National Academy of Television Arts and Sciences; National Academy of Recording Arts and Sciences' (MusiCare and Grammy in the Schools); the American Film Institute, the Society of Motion Picture & Television Engineers, Royal Television Society, and the Royal Photographic Society.

Springboard to Stardom: Start Locally

In order to springboard into the world of television production, I started locally in the cable television industry. With a little ingenuity and encouragement from my classmates, we formed the Collegiate Educational Television Association for graduate students majoring in education at Howard University in Washington, DC. My classmates assisted me in producing my own cable TV program, *"The Sonya Show"* Cable TV Special. For my productions, I videotaped educational programs, music videos, sports events, as well as business programs. I tried to be well rounded by focusing on a broad background in the fundamentals. The professor that was instrumental in me getting to do my educational television internship at a local cable station was Dr. Faustine Jones-Wilson.

Because I have never been one to wait around for someone to discover me and while most of my classmates were trying to get into the university's TV station for job placements, I decided to look for a job closer to my home. My search paid off quickly because a week before I graduated, the mayor's office in my suburban town needed a Cable TV Coordinator to manage their government and public access channel. I was hired, and while there refined my skills in producing an entire television show including scriptwriting, editing, producing, and post-producing. If you can name it, I did it.

Although in the late 1980's higher education had not made its mark in television and despite the fact that my graduate advisor had made it clear that the Sesame Street age group (preschoolers) were the only ones using educational television at that time, I pursued the field anyway. By the time of my graduation, the local junior college's TV department personnel came looking for higher education TV producers like me to serve on their new board of advisors for television training programs. These early TV training experiences led to the development of today's popular *telecourses* and served, in my county, as the beginning of college courses for credit and non-credit by way of cable TV.

Behind the Scenes Team

All celebrities need highly effective behind-the-scenes people including press agents, wardrobe attendants, make-up artist, photographers and many others. Of course my family and friends continue to play a vital part in my star power kingdom. What is a superstar without an effective team? My behind the scenes people are the best people in the world because I can always count on them. A key element in building a successful team is to develop relationships with people who care about me and share my goals even as I develop through life's different stages. We mutually share our goals with each other for clarity and encouragement, and we sincerely enjoy watching members of our group develop and succeed.

It is said that no man is an island, and I certainly don't take credit for my team's effectiveness. I was blessed with an excellent support team of administrators. Having relationships that empowered and strengthened me has been the key to my success. There are few things more valuable and more helpful in my journey towards stardom than having a support team of loyal and trusted family and friends. I have loyal childhood friends that have known me since kindergarten. My close and trusted friends and family members are the most important assets of my effective team. It is most helpful if you also have a recognizable name to become a celebrity as well.

Name Recognition

Never neglect the power of name recognition. One day, I had a little mishap with my car. I forgot to turn off the headlights and my brand new battery went dead. Although my home was only a few blocks from the subway's parking lot, I felt too tired and sleepy to walk, and I took a cab home. The next day when I walked to the corner market to get a cab back to the subway, coming out of a local convenient store were two subway workers in a company truck getting coffee. I approached the workers and asked if they had jumper cables? *"No"*, they replied and casually ignored me. I asked another question and by this time the driver began staring into my face as though I looked familiar to him.

He asked my name and had I worked as the city's Cable TV Coordinator. That was several years ago, but he remembered my last name [SWINTON] because he used to be the videographer for the local Boys & Girls Club sports events. He was also trained at my cable TV studio in one of my training classes. Without hesitation this time, they found the jumper cables and even waited for twenty minutes until my car's battery was fully charged before they departed for another work assignment. Name recognition is one of the first things any celebrity must possess in order to gain notoriety. Even mega-movie star Marilyn Monroe had her name changed for ultimate stardom success.

Cyberspace Celebrity

Technically speaking, cyberspace suits me just fine because I get to be featured on something called a large bandwidth, if you will. I am very excited about the future of the Internet's potential. Don't I just look like a celebrity? That's right, I agree! I am already a celebrity; people just don't know it, yet! But they will soon find out why. There are trade secrets to being a celebrity. The Star Power ingredients to become a celebrity are talent, attitude, publicity, fan club and wealth.

Talent

Not all celebrities in the film, music, theater or television industries have the same degree of talent, nor do they need a lot of talent. As it is said, talent is in the eye of the beholder or should I say casting director. Whatever your talent, you will have an audience, large or small, intimate or extravagant whether office buddies or classroom pals, your type of entertainment will entertain somebody. For the novice entertainer, I usually advise the individual to check out the type of audience that he or she would like to attract or would enjoy performing in front of, and I emphasize practice, practice and more practice. You will need to focus on your audience's taste, background and mood.

I also suggest that one not worry about how old or young you are. I have seen amateur two-year-old performers make adults laugh and cry just like the seasoned pros. I have also witness older adults engage the interest of the preschool set with ease– take for instance, Captain Kangaroo and Mr. Rodgers. Most recently, I had the opportunity to witness the seasoned General Andrew Chambers' impromptu speech captivate a small group of preschool and elementary school age children at a local Community Service program that I was hosting in the city's main library.

Attitude

As a creative visionary, I usually write my own rules, but if you want to make it in the entertainment industry, my advice is to start out playing the game by their rules. Your positive attitude and outlook towards change will be one of the biggest assets that leads to your success. If you are a novice or even if you are a seasoned pro, understanding and having the proper attitude when dealing with competitive people is important in the entertainment industry. It's important to understand this because one person's competitive nature could lead to another person's downfall in this business. My advice is to not waste your time in petty squabbles but that you should be compassionate and reserve all of your energy for a positive and productive life for yourself.

Publicity

"What makes great publicity", you ask? controversy, I feel that audiences are really captivated by madness and mayhem. Take for instance, Lisa (Left eye) Lopez of the famed Grammy award winning, recording group *TLC*. When her courtship to her then fiancé, professional football player Andre Rison, went haywire, she admittedly burned down his multi-million dollar mansion by angrily lighting a pair of tennis shoes with lighter fluid and leaving them in a ceramic bathtub to smolder. It seems as though her explosive behavior didn't stop the group's record sales from skyrocketing to the top of the Hip Hop and R&B charts. This erratic incident goes to show that controversy can definitely be one of the main ingredients to becoming an *interesting* overnight celebrity. However, I don't recommend burning the house down to get attention.

Although, extremely talented in his day, another example is former heavyweight, world champion boxer, Muhammad Ali. Ali caused a lot of controversy when he refused to carry out his military draft because of his Muslim religious beliefs. It was an exciting day for me to have met this world-class gentleman. Having adversaries is another ingredient. A close friend of mind once said that his adversaries have done more for his celebrity status than he could ever do with a savvy marketing and publicity team. He emphatically stated, *"call it free advertisement, if you will"*. He said for me to ask anyone who has ever been popular if they had adversaries and the answer is always, yes! (He expressed that the more popular you are, the more adversaries you will have– the *powerful* and not so *powerful* adversary).

Case in point, he exclaimed, "all *popular* people have adversaries". He suggested that the louder his adversaries are— the better. I asked him why did he need loud mouth adversaries? He jokingly said to me, *"because then he would not have to toot his own horn"*. *"That makes sense"*, I said. He chuckled as he explained that, *"with a loud mouth adversary"*, he could rest assured that they would unknowing and without restraint *broadcast* his name for him. He said to think of it this way; his adversaries have called out his name, more than he would have ever called out his own name. He emphasized that he just makes sure that his adversaries get the spelling of his name *correct*. He added, *"better still — it is not what his adversary says about him that matters the most, it is only how he reacts to what his adversary says, true or not."* With an assured grin he stated, *"my adversary's sharp-tongue arrows can't fool everyone."* I had to give him his due respect and accolades; at least he had his defensive strategy down to a fine science of the *perils of the adversary*.

A friend of mine told me that she once had a delightful art gallery manager that did not like her bold and provocative exhibit selection for their grand opening. Her supervisor used to send her to his boss's office in order to rid himself of her. Before an important exhibition, instead of her boss' supervisor reprimanding her for the specific selection of oil paintings, her art gallery got a cool write up from an art critic in the local daily newspaper's style section which in turn boosted sales and led to more clientele. After that encounter, her own reluctant manager even began to admire her show case selection of bold and vivid color schemes and even began to allow her to present the new exhibits to the art gallery's board of directors for recommendations of upcoming events. Not to mention he became an instant fan of hers.

Fan Club

What is a celebrity without a fan club? All celebrities have fan clubs. And an ordinary person like me also has a fan club. My dad and mom were the first president and vice-president of my fan club. My older sister, Scharyl, and I had stage names Ms. Vecee and Ms. Kessy. *"CBS the stars address"* is the motto we would chime in after the introductory commercial. We started a neighborhood fan club when I was five. My sister and I made play envelopes and wrote letters to ourselves and read them out loud to our parents, neighbors and playmates. My parents always said that don't forget that a fan club can make you or break you. I am most grateful to them and my team of mentors for charging up my fan club entourage. Eddie Faye Gates is one of the many mentors in my arsenal of successful role models. My team of mentors has brought me a wealth of pleasurable challenges as well as rewards and for them I am most humbled with gratitude.

Wealth

Wealth is one of the many aspects of a superstar. I have already come to realize that I am already wealthy. To me, being wealthy is having a life that you enjoy living with the people you love being around. For me, that is my trusted family and friends. Finding my European ancestry as well as my other African American relatives has been a great joy; I am graciously thankful to my cousin Terrence Montgomery in Los Angeles, California and Gary R.R. Swinton (Dingley Village) in Victoria, Australia *(www.swintonfamilysociety.org)* and numerous other relatives.

Recently, it was an honor and surprise to find out that I had royalty in my family. In the 1700's William Swinton, The Royal Surveyor to the Crown laid out the land of Georgetown, South Carolina. As a Scottish pioneer, he settled five plantations but died early and left his three young children orphans. Thanks to the extensive research of my distant relative Gary R. R. Swinton who has assisted me in finding my rich family heritage from the United Kingdom by way of Scotland.

As a descendant of the Royal Surveyor, we have formed the new Royal Swinton Society for the United States' American and African American Swintons. Our website is *www.royal-swinton-society.org*. In order that my relatives from all over the world can keep abreast of our family events in the United States as well as the United Kingdom and the other countries, please join us on the web at *www.swinton-family-society.org*. Yes, my family and friends have brought me fond memories and genuine joy as well as rewarding challenges.

Horizon and Beyond

Everyone is entitled to his/her own viewpoint of the power of the Internet. In the twenty-first century Internet broadcasting of film, music and television will become even more popular. I believe that there will be musicians, television and film stars that will be discovered first on the Internet. In an address at the Industry Luncheon at the 142 Society of Motion Pictures & Television Engineers, Jack Valenti, Chairman and CEO of the Motion Picture Association, stated that his organization is *"seriously committed to marketing movies on the Internet one day"*. I feel that this is a very positive outlook by a highly respected motion picture authority. Don't you agree? With this in mind, and now that you have the secrets of an Internet celebrity, what are you waiting for?

Anyone can be a celebrity in cyberspace. So go ahead and get yourself a website and become the famous starlet you always wanted to be. The only thing standing in your way is only a galaxy. If you are a small struggling entertainment agency of one and would like some insight on getting your organization recognized by the major contenders, then this book is for you. The Internet has leveled the playing field of large and small entertainment agencies and individuals. Now is the time to take stock of your business' services and products for the entertainment industry. Take great pride in your smallness. Consider it a plus.

Advertising, marketing and promoting your small organization to the entertainment industry has never before been tremendously available until now. If you are just getting started or if you are an old pro to the film, music, radio or television industry the world is yours for the asking. I have found that a number of individuals, smaller businesses and non-profit organizations need assistance in advertising, marketing and promoting their specialized projects and services. I also found that numerous large to midsize entertainment firms need the services of talented individuals, small businesses, and non-profit organizations.

This is where your entertainment services come in to fill a special niche. By sharing my tested and proven experiences and the experiences of other successful advertising and marketing experts, I hope to encourage and propel you to reach your full potential by reaching your most valued customers–time and time again via the internet. This resource book was prepared especially for the individual, non-profit organization or a small business of one for some area of needed insight of advertising, marketing or promoting. Please e-mail me your success stories at: *success-story—internet-celebrity.com* and be sure to visit me at *www.internet-celebrity.com.* The proceeds of this book are dedicated to my family's organization, the *Royal Swinton Society.* We are positive about our family's future generations and we hope to leave a legacy of rich family heritage for the continuation of our family's genealogical research. Please visit our family's website: *www.royal-swinton-society.org.*

Chapter 2

Advertising On the Internet

HELLO! Entertainment World of Cyberspace

There is now no doubt that the Internet really is the biggest gold rush of our lifetime. This chapter tells you how to get online, get an Internet presence that sells, and get your piece of the new Internet pie. My motto is, *"I'm Sonya D! Bringing you the key, to unlock your prosperous future, in the entertainment industry"*. It is time for you to stake a place on the World Wide Web for yourself, your children, and the generations that follow. Someday people will look back and judge us as one of two groups: those who didn't recognize the digital revolution and missed the greatest chance of our age, and those who smartly made a place for themselves in a new business model that will dominate the future.

Mark my word; it is unlikely you or I will get another opportunity as big as this one to earn huge profits anytime in the next 100 years. The World Wide Web is booming! Internet sales are growing by leaps and bounds, and even a dipping world economy can't make online entrepreneurs slow down or look back. Ninety-two million people in the United States and Canada surf the Internet. That's a whopping thirty percent jump in just one short year. People aren't just looking, they are also buying online. The number of online consumers has increased 40% in recent years to 28 million. Perhaps even more important, the number of women buying online went up 80% in the past nine months, reaching the 10 million mark.

The Art of Advertising Online

It is time to get on board, right now. The Internet is a gigantic place. Millions of people are shouting about billions of products. Online advertising is low cost, but it is also a little bit like yelling your message in a crowded, noisy outdoor rock concert. Try to advertise to everyone, and you will wind up getting the attention of no one. It's important to niche your marketing. Begin by deciding exactly who will be your best prospects and customers.

Even as a small entertainment business, you will have to decide to advertise first to a small group of specialized industry newsgroups. Observe the conversation in the chat rooms and throw out some of your own ideas. If you don't already have something to sell, start by looking for a big group that is online and needs help. After trying a few advertisement displays online, I found a large number of first-time entertainment websites needed help with marketing and promoting their entertainment business. They found that they couldn't get started without an advertising and marketing plan.

I suggest to my prospective clientele, whether they are in film, music, television, etc. to focus on market research. I find out where my target audience goes to find products and services. Ask yourself some thought–provoking questions such as: what kinds of websites do they visit? What e-mail newsletters do they subscribe to? What trade entertainment magazines do they read? Are they *Variety, Hollywood Reporter, Grammy Magazine*, and etc. These are some of the entertainment publications that you will use to market to your best prospects and clients. The more you know about your target audience, the better you will be able to reach them, and the bigger your sales will be. You can get information on customers by talking to them and by offering a questionnaire on your website or by e-mail. Give a free gift or special discount to those who complete your questionnaire. Good, precise targeting quadruples the effectiveness of your advertising and gets your cash register ringing.

Make your e-mail or website copy talk directly to your best customers. Use easy words and short sentences. Customers love to hear the benefits they will get after they buy from you. Talk about how the customers will save more, earn more, save time, or feel better. Provide examples or statistics that prove your claims. Include testimonials from satisfied customers. For example, *"Sonya can show you ways to turn your website into a cash-generating machine that turns visitors into buyers"*, says Gina Davis of Community TV USA Network.

Word of Caution About FREE Websites

Free web hosts are great for hosting a personal website, but not recommended for an entertainment or media business site. If you're really serious about your business and want to establish your Internet presence, I highly recommend you do some serious research before you begin. You'll be better off in the long run. After reviewing hundreds of websites over the past couple of years, I have come to the conclusion that many small business websites are missing the boat. For example, I've been working on a couple of clients' promotions and was searching for a simple targeted mailing list. I searched through about twenty sites and not one of those sites was, what I would consider, professional. Their standard blue links were enlarged to about a size 16 font, busy backgrounds, flashing images and very unorganized. Did I purchase a mailing list from any of those sites? Well, my answer is absolutely not. Why? The way I see it, if those companies don't take pride in their websites, chances are, they won't take pride in their products either. Large linked text and flashing graphics won't make sales.

Your website is a direct reflection of you and your entertainment small business. The appearance of your site is the most important factor in determining your site's value. In other words, if your site doesn't look professional or pleasing to the eye at first glance, its perceived value and the value of your products and services will be low. On the other hand, you may have a great well–designed website, and a quality product or service, but if it takes too long to load, the value will still be perceived as low. Why? Because your potential customer will not wait; ultimately costing you business.

Another consideration of great importance is your content. Not just links, but content with value. When someone is surfing the Internet and they visit your website, they're visiting for a reason. Your site has something they want. Whether it is your product, service or information, that's why they're there. If they don't find what they're looking for, they move on to the next site and so on. If you want your visitors to stay at your site, provide the quality content they're looking for in a nicely organized fashion. Give them a reason to want to explore your site and to continue to visit your site in the future.

After receiving many questions in regards to site design from Swinton International Enterprises clients, I have devised a list of what I refer to as *"Sonya's 20 Website Mistakes-Boo Boos"!*

Sonya's 20 Website Mistakes-Boo Boos

1. Poor overall appearance
2. No contact information
3. Spelling/Grammar mistakes
4. Poor load time
5. Busy, distracting backgrounds
6. Multiple banners and buttons
7. Large fonts
8. Pop up messages
9. Poor use of tables
10. Scrolling text in the status bar
11. Different backgrounds on each page
12. Poor navigation

13. Broken links and graphics
14. Large slow loading graphics
15. Too many graphics
16. Multiple use of animated graphics
17. Poor use of mouse over effects
18. Multiple colored text
19. Text difficult to read
20. No Meta tags

Take some time to really look at your site. Compare it to sites that you feel look professional. Time your site's load time. Your customers won't wait. Their time is very valuable! The simple, well-designed sites make the sales. If your sales aren't what you had hoped, take some time to seriously evaluate your website and make some changes before spending your time and money on advertising and marketing. You may be pleasantly surprised. If you're doing business on the Internet, one of the most important aspects of your success is your website. If your website doesn't look professional, no matter what product you're offering your chances of success are minimal. Before you begin, if you've never designed a web page, it would be wise to become familiar with HTML (Hypertext Markup Language).

"The page cannot be displayed." Have you ever encountered this message while surfing the net? Of course you have. We all have. Think it can't happen to you? Think again. If you're hosting your business on one of the free hosting services, you're literally placing your entire business in the hands of a complete stranger. Free hosting services don't need to have a reason to shut your site down. You may get up one morning, try to access your site and instead of your site loading, this message will appear, *"The page cannot be displayed."* There goes all of your hard work, your website, your traffic, your search engine positioning, your customers all gone.

To tell the truth, free hosting services aren't interested in your business or how hard you've worked to design your website and create a steady stream of traffic. Believe me, I know from experience because unfortunately it happened to me at the very beginning of Community TV USA Network's free promotional community photo program. Our promotion's department used to use *Zing.com* to host our free community photos— that was until their website server shut down on July 2, 2001. Their main concern is their business. That's why they're doing it. They display banner advertisements on every site they host. Pop-up advertisements are not only irritating, but they make your site appear to be unprofessional. In addition, many Search Engines will not allow free host URLs to be listed. If you're serious about your business and you have a sincere desire to succeed, having your own domain name is a must. It's not a luxury; it's a necessity!

Businesses using the free services are not taken seriously. Having your own domain name is just as important if not more important than a professional looking website. They go hand-in-hand. The cost to register your Domain name use to be $70 for the first two years and $35 per year there after but they can now be registered cheaper than that. It is very reasonable and well worth every penny. You can register your domain name with The InterNIC right online. The InterNIC is a cooperative activity between the U.S. Government and Network Solutions, Inc. Network Solutions, Inc. (NSI), is a provider of domain name registration services in the .com, .net and .org top-level domains. *http://www.networksolutions.com.*

Be sure to also have your own entertainment e-mail address. Time and time again, I receive business cards that read *www.name@hotmail*, *name@yahoo* after having an elaborate business card and website. This is tempting but it detracts from your professionalism. At the beginning of making your entertainment contacts, it is better to be overly professional looking than under prepared.

When selecting a professional web host, your first consideration should be the company. Check out your website's hosting service background. Talk to some of their customers and ask them if they've been satisfied with their service. How many customers do they serve? What is their uptime percentage? Do they require you to make payments in advance? Do they charge set up fees? How is their customer support? Do they offer fast connections, be sure to test them? Do they offer shopping cart software to process your orders? Can you upgrade free of charge? Web hosting prices vary greatly. When selecting your host, make sure you're getting exactly what you're paying for. Keep in mind, a lower monthly rate will not benefit you if your site is down a lot, slow, or customer service is poor.

Selecting a professional web host is a very important decision. Make sure you do your homework and ensure that the host you select offers exactly what you need. Your own domain name *(www.your-name.com)*. Your own True POP e-mail account—*name@your-domain.com*. Your own unrestricted cgi-bin, access to SSL Encryption for secure transactions Java, C, C++, Tcl support, auto responders, FPT access and password protection for your files or directories. Your host company should at least offer 1 GIGABYTE (1024 MB) of Daily Transfer Design (and upload to) your site using Netscape or other HTML editing software Microsoft FrontPage (98) Server Extensions. For those utilizing FrontPage, you should have unlimited free access to your server via Telnet/FTP Online in-voices, account tracking, and payment history to enable you to check your account balance, monthly invoices, past payments. They should also allow a complete daily server backup, easy access to your log files and statistics on visits to your site.

Sonya's Tips for Designing a Successful Website:

I started out in elementary school, earning to be a graphic artist. Boy! did I love Art class. I was one of Ms. Goodman's 9th grade prize students. I got so involved in art that I won first place in a local Art contest and someone purchased my acrylic painting entitled *"Our Town"*. Oh! sweet memories—well, back to the story. Here are my tips for designing a successful entertainment website.

The main page of your website should load in 8 seconds or less with a 56K modem. According two recent surveys, conducted by Forrester Research and Gartner Group, e-commerce sites are losing

$1.1 to $1.3 billion in revenue each year due to customers click-away caused by slow loading sites. If a page takes too long to load, your potential customer will not wait. Ultimately costing you business.

Make sure you include proper META tags in the HTML of each page of your website. META tags are HTML codes that enable the search engines to determine what keywords are relevant to a specific site. About 80 percent of all website traffic originates from the eight major search engines. It would be a good idea to make sure you've done your homework and fully understand how to optimize your web pages prior to designing your site; this will save you a lot of headaches in the long run.

Be cautious when selecting your background and text colors. Busy backgrounds make text difficult to read and draw the attention away from the text. Always be consistent with your background theme on each page of your site. Your site should be nicely organized and uniform throughout. Keep in mind, colors affect your mood and will have an affect on your visitors as well. Bright colors such as yellow and orange, cause you to become more cheerful or happy, while colors such as blue and purple have a calming effect. Dark colors such as brown and black have a depressing effect. A good rule of thumb would be to use colors based upon the type of effect you're trying to achieve.

Use minimal animated graphics. These can be very distracting and can cause your page to look unprofessional. In addition, animated graphics cause your page to load more slowly. Fancy graphics won't make the sale. Your main page should specifically let your visitors know exactly what you're offering. How many times have you visited a site and never figured out exactly what they were selling? If your potential customer can't find your product or service, they definitely won't waste a lot of time looking for it. They'll go on to the next site and probably never return. They're visiting your site for a specific purpose. They want something your site offers. Whether it is information, a product or service. Try to avoid placing banner exchange advertisements at the top of your page. These can instantly take your customers or even be indexed by search engine robots. Limit the number of banners on your site to no more than two per page. One is ideal.

Always include your contact information on each page of your site and try to reply to all comments and suggestions within 48 hours. This will help promote good business relationships. Your business relationships are the key to your success. Always check and double-check your site for spelling errors and make sure your images and links are all working properly. If you have several errors, this will make your site appear to be unprofessional. If you are designing your site using an HTML editor, use spell check.

Proper grammar is also very important. If you've been out of school for a while, like me, it's probably a good idea to refresh your memory. Get a qualified editor. Design your site to be easily navigated. Place your navigation links together at the top, bottom, left or right side of the page. Use tables to neatly align your links. If you are planning on using graphic buttons to navigate your site, keep in mind that with each graphic you add to your page, it will take that much longer for your page to load. With only a handful of navigational links at your disposal, using graphic buttons will be fine. It would be wise to simply use text links to keep your load time down. Use Frames sparingly. Frames, if not properly used, can make your site look unprofessional. Avoid making your visitors have to scroll from side to side to view your content. This can be very irritating and cause your visitors to leave. If you must use frames, offer your visitors a choice. Frames versus No Frames.

Try to keep the number of clicks required to get from your main page to any other page on your site down to four. Keep in mind: Your visitors may enter your site from pages other than your main. Always have good navigational links on every page and place your company logo on each page. There are many advantages associated with the use of auto responders. Not only do they automate the daily task of manually replying to requests for information, but also they provide instant gratification for the recipient. They also enable you to track your ad responses and gather the e–mail addresses of potential customers. A good auto responder service will automatically send you an e–mail notification informing you each time someone requests your information.

When selecting an auto responder service, there are many factors that need to be taken into consideration to ensure maximum perform-ance: *Personalized Responses*– this makes the recipient feel that the letter was sent specifically to them; *Automatic Follow-ups*, studies have shown it may take up to seven contacts before closing a sale; *Unlimited Text Length*– if you are inhibited by the amount of text your auto responder may contain, you may be forced to revise a successful sales letter; *Free Unlimited Updating* is imperative in order to provide your customers with the most accurate, up to date information on your products and services; *Automatic Notification*– you must have the abil-ity to track your advertisement performance. You should be instantly informed each time someone requests your information.

The Affiliate Program

After you've created your product, consider setting up an affiliate program for massive distribution. There are many affiliates CGI scripts available to assist you in running your own affiliate program (The Affiliate Program at *www.theaffliateprogram.com).*

If you're selling a service on the Internet, you can offer your poten-tial customers a free trial as well. For example, if you offer a search engine submission service, you can provide your customers with a limited free submission to the search engines. To entice your cus-tomers to purchase your full service you can, not only submit their site to your full list of search engines, but you can also create doorway pages, insure their pages are optimized for the search engines and pro-vide a resubmission service every month for a year. In addition, pro-vide your clients with a free report of each submission process.

Prior to doing your customers last submission, contact them and inform them that their submission contract will soon be expiring. Tell them how they can renew their submission process and offer another enticing freebie such as, *"If you renew your submission contract before*

(date) we will also submit your site to over 1000 Free For All Sites." This
type of free trial will not only increase your current sales, but it will
promote future sales as well. The possibilities are endless. By offering
your potential customers something of value for free, providing
instant gratification, and an easy ordering process, you can dramati-
cally increase your sales.

On the Internet, a good website can make you as big as any corporation. You can get a good designer to develop a logo, some buttons, and
a background that looks right for your business. Then build your own
web pages around the elements the designer has given you. This is an
excellent way to get an eye popping website for as little as $100. Don't
get too carried away with bright colors, patterned backgrounds, or big
graphics that can take time to load. Recent surveys show that over 78%
of your customers will be using slower dial-up modems past 2002.
Slow loading pages discourage visitors who often click away before
they have even had a chance to consider your offer. If your site is getting hits, but not making any sales, slow loading pages could be causing the problem. Basic colors and a white background do best with the
many different ways your page will look on different monitors.

Use headlines and subheadings to give customers a quick idea of
what your page has to offer. Someone in a hurry should be able to read
your headlines and subheadings to quickly understand what entertainment products, services, and/or benefits they will get. Be sure to
put your most important phrases in *bold* letters, stay away from all
capitals in your writing, and use common fonts that are legible. Above
all, try to include testimonials from your customers and suppliers
when you can. Nothing builds trust with customers and prospects like
good words about you from people who know you and have done
business with you.

I believe that a good entertainment website must be easy to navigate with links to important pages included on every page.
Furthermore, the look and feel of your website should be consistent. In
addition, you can do this by using the same logo, background, type
style, and navigation buttons on every page. A website is the perfect

place to display your entire entertainment product and service catalog without having to bear the high cost of printing and mailing. More over, you can build your own professional catalog fast with a few mouse clicks by using the online catalog too.

Research has shown that search engines are the number one way of getting visitors to your site. You will need pages that are easily registered by the top search engines like Excite and Yahoo. Search engines are a lot smarter than they used to be. Most search engines first look at the title of your page (those words that appear in the little box on your browser), then at the page's Meta Tags, and finally at the copy on your page. If the same keywords appear in all three places, your site gets a high listing. This means that a customer who searches for you using one of your site's keywords will find you linked in the first 10 to 15 sites the search engine presents. To see what Meta tags look like, go to any popular site, point your cursor at the page, and click the right mouse button. Choose *"view source."* The Meta tag looks like this: <meta name-="description" content="a few words that best describe your site, separated, by, commas"> <meta name="keywords" content="the same keywords listed like this: internet marketing, small business, website promotion, selling, e–zines, home based business, marketing, advertising, e-mail marketing,">. Be sure to update your important information often. Search engines, just like customers, check back often to see how your site is progressing. The use of helpful articles, tips, and a question and answer page will give customers needed valuable information. Also, include links to other recommended sites like yours. Try to get those sites to add to your link as well. Customers will see you as an authority in your field and will appreciate your ability to help them in a variety of ways.

Your own domain name will make your business look bigger and your Internet effort more serious. *Yourname.com* looks a lot more impressive than a free website address, and don't forget to include all your contact information where customers can easily find it. This will also include your phone, fax, and your regular mailing address. For best results, a street address will add more credibility to your website.

Invite visitors to e-mail you with questions and for more information. Did you know that people on the Web like to make purchases with speed and convenience?

I would like to emphasize that you learn all the details on how you can get your own credit card forms and automated ordering with CGI scripts at *www.HomeBusiness-Mag.com*. In this way, you will be able to assure your customers that their credit card information is secure, safe, and private. Include your fax number, toll free phone number, and mailing address for those who prefer to order via those methods. After your customer buys something, follow up with an e-mail confirming the order. Tell your customer the total price of their order and when their product will be sent. According to *Investor's Business Daily*, many corporations are finding this kind of follow-up is the number one reason customers come back to buy again.

I have concluded that one of the best things about a website is that it can make the Internet your extended staff. This is an invaluable boost if you are a one person entertainment business or a non-profit organization. Your website is there to answer questions at any time of day or night. Your web pages can fill in the additional information that your ad couldn't cover, your sales letter didn't have room for, or you forgot to mention in your telephone conversation. Many top television network marketers use websites to train new members and distribute announcements to their down line. They report it works much faster, better, and cheaper than sending out letters or spending hours on long distance. Include your website and e-mail address on all of your printed and off-line marketing materials. The corporate world spends most of their Internet advertising budgets promoting their websites on TV, radio, newspapers and magazines. Notice how the United Parcel Service (U.P.S.) now features the company website in the same big letters it uses to list its 1-800 number on all of the delivery trucks.

It may go without saying, but I'll stress to you anyhow—be sure to put your Internet information on your business cards, in-voices, letterhead, and voice mail. Look into advertising your website in affordable and targeted entertainment magazine advertisements, on radio, and in cable TV commercials. Try to get *free* big media promotion. Almost all e-zine, TV, radio, newspaper, and magazine editors accept press releases. Now that most media sources are online, e-mail is the preferred way for them to receive your press releases. Your release should be one page long and offer valuable information of interest to the publications' readers. Editors won't print a blatant ad that is not accompanied by newsworthy information.

Profitable Advertising Techniques

The 2001 advertising sales slowdown has made a lot of commercial television networks and radio stations nervous because this has caused a negative impact on the media conglomerates' revenue. Not to mention that the stock shareholders in the telecommunications/ media sector have caused quiet a bite of future trading uncertainty. For instance, this would normally be a busy time of year for my colleague Barbara Vassi, but business has been slower than usual. She worries things will get even slower in the months ahead. With this in mind, Greg Ford, her business partner came up with a terrific idea for building a second income from the Internet. Months later, his website and advertising have only brought in a few sales. He was afraid that all his time, money, and enthusiasm were wasted. I hear similar experiences from dozens of people each week with this same problem; some are startups, others are mature businesses. I speculate that most first time business ideas flop on the first try, but the key to success is knowing how to give yourself a big second opportunity. Sometimes you will need to try a third or fourth time before your new product or service brings home the bacon. Here are some simple ways to give your entertainment business a better opportunity for success.

Try to give your business a tighter focus. Many businesses are too broad, trying to interest too many different kinds of prospects. Being too general will leave you lost in a crowd. America has more stores than at any time in history. Retailers are finding their markets split into tiny fragments as shoppers have a bewildering choice of places to spend their money. Meanwhile, the Internet is exploding. Christmas spending in 2000 is 2.3 Billion dollars, twice what it was in 1999. All that money is divided among some 300 million web sites. How do you compete when there are so many others? Tighten your business focus to include a narrow, very well–defined audience. The man who sells John Denver memorabilia from the 1970s has a very specific, almost peculiar business. But he is selling his product like crazy on the Internet. He is filling a niche that deeply interests a particular group of people.

Try to make your prices more competitive. For the past few years, consumers have told us that they want quality and service with price being much less important. Now consumers are ranking *price* as one of the most important reasons they buy from one business and not from another. Think of ways you can tighten your belt or redefine your product or service to offer it at a lower cost. Maybe you can limit your service to fewer, but still important features. Perhaps your prices are already lower than competitors. If this is your situation, I suggest that you may just need to emphasize your lower prices more in your marketing campaign. Definitely starting in 2001, lower prices are suddenly an important way to get people to buy.

Another idea is to be sure to choose the product or service that sells best for you, and then expand it. Try using the *"go wide and sell deep"* method. This simply means to offer more versions of the same entertainment product or service. For example, if your musical CD (vocal version) is selling well, then come out with an instrumental version of the same CD, and furthermore, look for more related products or services you can offer. For instance, I first started out writing press releases for media companies, and I have found that those same companies wanted me to write promotional articles for them as well; that became a related service I could offer along with my popular press release service.

Another idea is to sharpen your entertainment marketing materials so that they will standout in a crowded classified advertisement carrying the same products and services. With all that competition in the entertainment business world, you profit when your marketing and advertising stands out and hits home with consumers. Give all your marketing pieces a headline. Busy prospects need a way to quickly find out *"what's in this for me"* before they will take the time to read your sales letter, brochure, classified ad, or website. Relate the features of your product or service to the benefits the buyer will get. If your Internet *"music video"* has a clever dial-on-demand button, tell your prospects how your dial-on-demand button will save them time, money, and make their day more enjoyable. You see, it is the *benefits* that your buyers really care about. Take a closer look at where you are putting your advertising dollars. It can be very tempting to place all your cash into commercial media that will instantly reach a lot of people, but are all those people your best prospects?

The experts suggest that marketing is generally more effective when it can be *closely* targeted to a well-defined audience. If your audience is made up of your best customers, you get sales. Consider advertising in the entertainment trade publications, the e-mail newsletters, and on entertainment websites. Another convenient avenue of marketing is to market using one-sided postcards. This is considered clever because postcards are cheap and prospects read them without having to open an envelope.

Last but not least, try to expand your promotional efforts. It takes quite a bit of advertising, marketing, and promotion to get into the heads of your busy prospects. Busy entertainment executives and account representatives are constantly bombarded with ads and commercials. You need to hit your best prospects over and over again before your message sinks in. Look for several ways you can consistently market your small entertainment business. In addition, try to find affordable methods that reach your best customers and use those methods over and over again. When marketing doesn't work, it is almost always because the business ran out of money and gave up too soon. Give your business another opportunity to succeed. The children's story of the *"little engine that could"* might as well be a $1,000 business seminar. The best way to clobber competition and build your business into a cash cow is to give your business a tight focus, make prices more competitive, expand what works, improve marketing materials, and promote big and consistently.

I Heard It Through the Grapevine-
Put Sound On Your Website

I have a good friend, who is also a musician by the name of Ivan Taylor of Multi-pro. He owns a wall-to-wall digital entertainment system in his apartment to record his musical CDs. It was a good thing he could write and play his own instruments because he put up his own Internet radio station, and so can you. He now sales his very own CD's around the world this way.

Sound and video has come to the Internet in a big way. Now, with cheap new technology, anyone can turn their website into a TV or radio station without spending a dime. Given the huge audiences that radio and TV have (99 percent of American homes have a TV and most own five radios), putting audio and video on your site could be the most important thing you can do. Some studies show audio and video can increase website sales by as much as 50 percent. Streaming media, as it is called, excites customers and keeps you ahead of your competition. The static printed web page will be around for a long time, but watch for most leading sites to start offering audio and video. Streaming media requires a lot more data than a simple printed page. Having DSL or a T line helps. Since most consumers still use dial-up modems on lines that support less than 40k, Internet audio and video rely on clever methods for compressing and reducing big files of data.

The result is sometimes fuzzy audio and pictures that look faded and blurry. The level of quality might be annoying on regular TV, but it's nothing short of exhilarating coming from the Internet. One client who is using web video says he is getting a phenomenal rate of sales from it. Your website visitors won't mind a bit if your presentation isn't network professional. They will appreciate the big jump from reading text to seeing a media presentation; I suggest that you start with audio. There is a huge difference between the amount of work it takes to produce video and what is needed to build an audio only presentation. A single individual can produce an outstanding radio show while even a simple TV program requires a full staff.

An audio presentation doesn't require location, lighting, or the inconspicuous microphone placement video demands. You can record your voice, add some music, drop in a sound effect and your audio program is ready to hit the Internet. There are a number of cheap or free programs that let you record your audio as a simple WAV file, a Real Audio file, or a an MP3. After trying several of them, a colleague of mine settled on a $20 program called Internet Audio Mix available from *www.acoustica.com*. It works with your PC's sound card to record up to four digital tracks. Operation and editing is completely intuitive. Most recent PCs have Real Audio bundled with windows. That means a large and growing number of your customers can click on your audio link, download your Real Audio file, and listen to it within a matter of seconds. So, be sure to speak with energy when you record your audio tracks because people will not be able to see your face, and your voice will be the only thing carrying your message to your potential customer. Try also to cut down on *uhs* and *uhms*. Don't feel like you have to talk like an announcer. Some audio buffs say that their customers respond better to a voice that sounds like a regular person. Several companies have created easy systems for producing and hosting your audio for free.

SONYA-The Video Diva

I suggest that you put some video on your website if you can. Although experts tell me that we're years away from having quality streaming video on the Internet. I still believe that there are some easy ways to offer fairly good video from your website. Because the Real Video format is becoming so widely accepted, you can download and use several of *www.RealNetwork.com's* free video production applications. Real Slideshow (free) lets you combine images with talk, music, and sound effects. Real Presenter (also free) turns your PowerPoint presentations into Internet video. Several of the free web hosting sites now hosts your streaming media presentations at no charge *www.Tripod.com*, one of the pioneers in free websites, offers a program called ShowMotion. You can combine still photos with clips of video, scanned images, and backed with your narration.

Tripod hosts it for free. If all this sounds a bit too technical, Tripod features several fine presentations produced by high school students. The format is a drag and drop system which impressed me as being vastly easier than designing a website. Even though Internet audio and video is a cutting-edge and exciting technology, it doesn't come near the quality we are used to with regular radio and television. But consider this information as good news for small entertainment websites. You can turn out a homespun effort and still be right on the heels of professionals

For more professional level video, check out *www.wbcimaging.com*. They are television engineers who have long taken an interest in the best ways to put video on the Internet. Although radio is a billion dollar industry, I still will affirm that television is arguably the most influential media ever invented. Now that it has become so easy to produce your own Internet audio and video, it makes more sense than ever to add those powerful dimensions to your website.

Sonya's Super Advertising Strategy
Pay-Per-Performance Advertising

Traditionally, advertising used to utilize a hit or miss kind of an approach. You would simply place your advertisement in a trade magazine, and then you would have to wait for the results several days or weeks later. If new customers didn't come through the door, you had little choice but to revise your ads and try again until you got it right. Large and small businesses using this kind of approach ended up facing major financial problems in the long run with this kind of haphazard technique. You could invest a lot of money before sales started coming in. Now, the new crop of Pay-Per-Performance advertising methods on the Internet give you results or you don't pay.

Instead of paying to place your advertisement, you pay for each lead your advertisement produces. You can adjust your ad, your media, and your method until prospects start to roll in. Only when you get results do you start paying small fees per lead. One of the quickest ways to pull lots of prospects to your website is to get listed prominently in search engines. Unfortunately, with over one billion sites catalogued, your URL can get lost in the crowd. Pay-Per-Performance search engines give you a way around this problem. They list your site high for a fee. You can pay as little as a penny a click for each prospect the engine sends to your site. If no one clicks on your link, you don't pay. The up side to these engines is you can adjust your listing until it works without going into debt. You can also list dozens, even hundreds of keywords that will bring up your link. The big disadvantage to Pay-Per-Performance search engines is that many keywords get very little response. Common keywords that draw lots of prospects are probably well known to other businesses in your industry. With everyone vying for the same keywords, the price can be bid up to several dollars per click. Some top Pay-Per-Performance search engines are *GoTo.com, NetFlip.com, FindWhat.com, Search-Hound.com,* and *RocketLinks.com.* Most require a $25 to $50 minimum to participate.

Pay-Per-Performance banner advertising is also popular. With banner response trending lower in recent years because businesses are now looking for ways around costly *cpm* banner purchases that don't always get results. Services like *ValueClick.com* and *PennyWeb.com* make you pay only when someone clicks on your banner and goes to your site. This strategy works well when you develop an eye-catching banner that gets your target audience to click to your website. You can increase your customers' responses by centering your banner a round graphics that help make your point. You can also add moving animation to your banner to grab even more attention. Be sure to keep your banner's file size down for rapid loading.

The newest innovation in Pay-Per-Performance advertising may well be the best idea yet. New *CustomLead.com* uses innovative banner ads to collect the e-mail addresses of your target customers. Prospects enter their e-mail address to receive information on your business. You pay only for unique confirmed email sign-ups. The point is to build your own opt-in e-mail list. You own the list and can use it indefinitely to e-mail updates, send out new offers, and distribute information to your prospects and customers.

Rather than a one-shot ad campaign, you can continue to work your list for weeks, months, even years getting the rich results repetition provides. The great advantage to CustomLead's Pay-Per-Performance advertising method is that it revolves around e-mail, by far the most popular feature of the Internet. While as few as 30% of the population surf websites, almost everyone with a computer at home or work uses e-mail. You reach prospects in a way people notice and respond to.

By using the big three kinds of Pay-Per-Performance advertising— search engines, banners, and e-mail— you stretch your ad budget with guaranteed results. You also have the ability to analyze hard statistics that render your results crystal clear. Perhaps most importantly, Pay-Per-Performance lets you focus your marketing plan on getting results rather than just increasing awareness. Not only do people learn your company's name, you also get the guaranteed result of an interested prospect seeing your full offer either at your site or in an e-mail.

Money, Money and More Money!
How to Make Money Online

Karen walked next door from her office to mine to announce she had finally resigned from her dead end job of administrative assistant. *"But I'm not ready for the senior citizens nursing home yet,"* she said. *"I want to make a living on the Internet. What can I sell?"* This is a question many of us struggle with as we see money, freedom, and a bright future for those who manage to find their niche online. You may have tried to sell something from the Internet only to find it is difficult to get visitors to your website and even harder to get them to buy. The biggest hurdle is simple: most folks are trying to sell products to the *individual* consumers. Allow me to emphasize to you that *that's not where the money is.* It is a more daunting task than most people realize.

Only one percent of retail sales happen on the Internet. Even though selling to consumers should be gargantuan one day, we have a long way to go before the majority of people are placing orders on the Internet. Instead, sell something to businesses. I do marketing and promotions for my own company, Swinton International Enterprises on BarterNet.com (formerly *Allbusiness.com* sponsored by American Express). This is a barter network for *business-to-business* transactions. Bartering is a multi-billion dollar business and I will give you some insight on the business of bartering in a later chapter. While individual consumer sales amounted to $20 billion last year, business-to-business purchases vaulted to a whopping $100 billion.

Clearly, if you want the easiest path to tapping into the land-slide of Internet cash, sell your entertainment product or service to another business. So, you say, *"I should sell a product to businesses?"* Not exactly. Most products need to be sold in large volumes by many distributors before they turn a profit. Chances are that hundreds or even thousands of other affiliates are also pushing the same product you also sell. In the end, many business buyers will simply click to the main corporate site to make their purchase. Your best bet for starting a small entertainment Internet business and earning a living online is to sell an entertainment *service* to businesses.

Unlike products, it is hard to mass-produce a service. Most service providers find their competition is relatively thin. This is especially true if you provide a very specialized service or do your job in a particular way that is hard to duplicate. Because entertainment services require time spent by an experienced expert, rates can be higher, especially for business customers. *"But I'm not an expert in anything people on the Internet would want to buy,"* you exclaim. This is not true.

Sit down with a pen and jot down all the things that you were paid for during your work career. Add to your list things you have done on your own time that friends, neighbors, or co-workers have felt were valuable. Which of these things could be sold on the Internet? If you tune pianos, give guitar or voice lessons; then you can sell your creative services to the vast number of small internet businesses who don't have the time or expertise to manage their own growing firm. If you produced your entertainment group's newsletter for several years, your desktop publishing and editing skills could fill the hot demand for people who can write and publish e-messaging campaigns, websites, and print newsletters. Best of all, an entertainment writer/editor deals in pure information, which is the easiest and cheapest to deliver over the Internet.

Take for instance, my neighbor Larry, who decided his skills from a career in graphic arts, would be hard to sell on the Internet. But he knew lots of things businesses needed and he had a list of town residents who could fill those needs. If you don't readily have an entertainment service you can sell to business, find someone who does. Many in-demand people don't have the time or know how to market themselves on the Internet. For example, my friend Alan is an entertainment and fashion photographer in which my company represents his services online; therefore we attracts a commission for each sale he makes.

Put up your own website with some articles that your business customers will find useful. This can serve several purposes by showing you know plenty about your line of work. You can post testimonials of your satisfied customers or from other experts in your industry. In order to get the full impact, be sure to list the person's full name and the name of their business or city they live in. Better still, you could offer to your customers and prospects a monthly update letter via e-mail. Include brief updates on important developments in the industry. In addition, you could mix in three lines of advertising to promote your services. I feel that selling a service to business is your least expensive way to get started making money online. It is also the quickest way to tap into the huge amounts of money traveling from business to business. Another crafty method of successful advertising is using *headlines* on your website.

How to Energizing Your Internet Advertisement

Every one of your marketing tools needs a headline. Headlines get attention, make your message easy to read, get your main selling points across, and lead your customer to a sale. Use a short three-word headline for classified advertisements. Use headlines frequently in your website copy to help people get your main message without having to spend a lot of time online. Headlines range from newspaper, *"hit-you-in-the face,"* to more subtle ones that don't seem like a headline at all. A hard-sell direct mail letter might have your headline in all capitals at the beginning. Or your headline can be softer and less obvious, more like an important paragraph in bold at the beginning of your letter. Here's something I know you will be interested in.

Your headline gets attention when it appeals to the reader's interests. For example, *"Omega Recording Studio can save you 40% on your first CD recording"*. Use your headline to point out a problem the reader has or something you know the reader feels strongly about. Headlines aren't a good place to list the features of your product or service. Instead, headline the benefit the feature provides. *"Web buster gets your site listed high on search engines. Nothing drives a flood of eager customers to your site faster."* Studies show headlines get even better results if they're enclosed in quotation marks like the example no page 43. It's a good trick to use from time to time. Here are several surefire headlines over the years copy writing pros have found useful. Several headline formulas that almost always work well. Try these headlines, putting your product, service, or benefit in place of mine.

1. Ask a Question. "Are you worried about filing your tax return this year?" A question headline gets the reader to answer in their mind. You automatically get the prospect involved in your message. Many people will read further into your letter, ad, or web site copy just to find out what answer or solution you provide.

2. Start your headline with "How to." *"How to Audition for Your very first commercial and Win a Call back."* "How to" headlines work like magic. Almost all my copyeditor friends say that they like their articles to start with "how to" because they have found that people love information that shows them how to do something valuable. It works for reports or letters that provide helpful information.

3. Provide a testimonial. The recommendation of a satisfied customer can go a long way in convincing others to buy from you. *"Robert Swinton's acoustic guitar lessons are fast and easy to learn!"* Mark Smith, Key West, Florida. Always include the customer's full name and the city they live in. Many readers won't believe a testimonial where it's hard to figure out who the author is. "R.A., L.A." doesn't work nearly as well as, "Richard Allen-Big Town, LA."

4. Issue a command. Some classic headlines command readers to *"Aim High"* and *"Put a tiger in your tank."* Turn your most important benefit into a commanding headline. *"Stop rushing through life." "Make more money this month." "Feel better about yourself."* Important news makes a good headline. This particularly works well for big changes in your company or the introduction of hot new products. *"Richard Benson is taking the helm as our new CEO with a powerful vision for the future." "Software Central introduces the new Instant Forms 2002—professional website forms in 20 minutes."*

5. Headline a deadline for a special offer. Most of us are busy and tend to put off taking action. If you don't get the prospect to act now, you may never get the sale. *"Save Money now"* and *"Get More If You Buy now,"* offers increase response.

6. Free offers often pull the best response. *"Free reports on boosting website sales,"* is a powerful way to get more interested prospects. There is a myth that affluent or professional customers are turned off by free offers. Not true. Simply tailor your free offer to match the style of your customers or industry. You might subtly

headline, a *"no-cost initial consultation," or ,"a bonus for the first customer." Remember that prospects* are in a hurry. They are bombarded with hundreds of ads, letters, postcards, and commercials every day. They tend to skip or tune out any marketing message that looks like it will take too much time or be too much trouble to figure out. Headlines simplify the learning curve. A reader can scan down your page, quickly digest your headlines, and figure out what you're offering. Once the prospect knows you have something she is interested in, she will take more time to read your entire letter, ad, or web page.

7. Spice your headlines with action words: save, act, run, feel, and do. Cut out unnecessary words. Put sub-headings in your copy to break up stretches of text. If someone else is writing copy for you, share some of these power headline ideas with him or her. In our hustle, bustle world, good headlines make your sales materials stand out, easy to use, and motivating.

Powerful Advertisement

Now that you have a powerful advertising campaign, I can give you several efficient ways to manage lots of customer questions, orders, and e-mail. Once your on-line entertainment business starts getting attention and pulling in sales, your workload will increase. Customers will ask questions, orders will fly in, and e-mail will invariably start to stack up. Much of use e-mail well. Use a signature (sig) file on all of your e-mail messages. Thirty million people use e-mail every day, so it makes sense to pack your messages with a special dose of promotion. A sig file is a four to six line message at the end of your e-mail. It contains your business name, a brief line about what you do and what benefit you bring to customers, your website address, and your contact info.

A sig file can be a good and acceptable source of advertising when posting to otherwise noncommercial UseNet Newsgroups. Find a news-group that discusses your area of expertise. Post a message offering useful information or answering a question. Your sig file can direct people back to you and your website for additional help. I like to send prospects my online color business card. I have found that it can work wonders for long distance introductions. Say for instance-Scotland. That's right, I use my online business card to introduce myself to national and international colleagues of the Royal Television Society. This way, meeting Roger Carter of the American RTS and Tony Currie, Chairman of the Royal Television Society-Scottish Center was a breeze. Now I will go on to handling the rush of responses.

Now that you have done all this promotion, don't be surprised if you wake up to find your e-mail box brimming with questions and orders from dozens or hundreds of customers. You will need an informed and organized way of smartly working leads and sales. Follow-up is key to selling. Some customers need seven to 10 contacts with you before they buy. This can increase sales 50%. If you are busy answering e-mail from a flood of new customers, it can be hard to find the time or remember to keep up with those you have already made contact with. Fortunately, e-mail offers a nearly free way to repeatedly follow-up with interested prospects.

Let an auto responders do the work for you. These simple online gizmos send your sales information to anyone who sends an email to your auto responder address. The auto responder then sends your customer additional messages and reminders at intervals, which you determine. A prospect could get your free report on day one, your sales letter on day two, and your special price list on day three. A week later your auto responder could send them a reminder with another message set to go out next month. All this is done automatically without you ever having to lift a finger.

Auto responders are one of the top promotional tools available online today. They are also known as mailbots, automatic email and email on demand. They were derived from the very popular fax on demand and designed to automatically respond to any email message sent to it with an automatic response. Their popularity most likely stems from its vast variety of uses as it eliminates the need to manually answer every response. Subsequently, saving hours of valuable time. Your information can be available to your prospective customer 24 hours a day, 7 days a week. Get your best ad copy ready, load it to your auto responder and your business is set to auto-pilot. When your prospective customer sends a message to your auto responder address, your information will be instantly delivered to their e-mail address.

There are many ways of utilizing the power of auto responders: sample e-zine copy for potential subscribers, articles for publication– A great way for entertainers or entertainment contractors to distribute their articles is to offer free reports on various entertainment subjects and use your signature file at the end to promote your website or business. Also, offer free resources with information about your site, product or business, and offer information about your business opportunity.

Sonya's Internet Advertising Tips:

Include your auto responder address in your signature file. When placing classified ads, instead of supplying your regular e-mail address, use your auto responder address. Join appropriate News Groups, opt in e-mail discussion lists, include a guest book register, display online business cards, letterhead logo, and your website address and don't forget to key code your advertisements.

Tracking your advertising response rate will be the key to your marketing success. Once you test your ads and determine which advertisement is pulling the most responses, you can easily test which classified ad sites are producing results as well. This will save you a lot of valuable time by only placing your ads at classified ad sites that produce results. Make a numbered list of the classified advertisement websites you intend to have your advertisement post.

You can key your advertising using the subject of your e-mail. Many times, if you ask for a certain *subject* description, it may not be provided. To avoid this problem you can add a simple code to your e–mail tag.mailto: *music@yourautoadd.com?subject=cla* this code should contain your auto responder address and will automatically fill in the subject with your ad key when clicked on. The *cla* stands for the classified ad site number one. The second ad site you have listed should be coded as *clb* or classified ad site number two and so on. By coding your ads you will know exactly where your leads are coming from. Begin submitting your ad and replace your normal e-mail address with your key coded auto responder address. You can obtain free auto responders with all the amenities I mentioned above from any of the following sites: *www.getresponse.com, www.fastfacts.net* and *www.myreply.com.*

E-mail programs like Eudora and Pegasus let you quickly route messages into files on your computer. Our account representative says that he keeps three files titled, *"Waiting for Order," "Fill Order,"* and *"Bill 'Em.."* You can also set up templates with answers to questions you get all the time. Instead of typing the same answer to a question over and over, you can click a button and the answer appears. This saves you many hours otherwise spent doing e-mail chores. Market, test, market, test. Few, if any, ideas work perfectly the first time. Look at any failures as learning experiences and as steps you take toward success. Test your products, services, and marketing. Analyze the results, make adjustments, and try again. You can track the effectiveness of advertising by directing respondents to a special email address or web page. For example, have them reply to *music2@classified.com.*

Affordable Internet Advertising

You've heard the old saying, *"It takes money to make money."* They might as well include *"It takes big money to make big money."* The local car dealership that always has a TV commercial on the evening news may be spending a million dollars or more each year to get those ads. So what's a small or home-based entertainment business or individual to do? How can you get *affordable* advertising that really works? The answer is, when your budget is tight, use classified advertisements.

These small ads come in a variety of sizes, costs, and appear everywhere from neighborhood newsletters to big national magazines to websites on the Internet. Classifieds really work. You can grab important prospects, get new customers, sell your products and services, but *only if* you know how to smartly use classified advertisement. Here are some simple things you can do today to make your classified advertisement sell:

Target your best prospects. While this might sound like marketing mumbo-jumbo, it's by far the most important way to make ads work. Every newspaper, newsletter, and website has its own particular kind of audience. Your advertisement won't sell unless your product or service is something that the publication's particular audience would buy. To figure out the audience a publication is reaching, look at their articles and ads. What kinds of businesses are advertising? What sorts of things are they selling? What group of people would buy these things? Think about age, gender, lifestyle, income, and level of education. It won't take long before you have a pretty good idea of what kinds of prospects the publication reaches. The Wall Street Journal attracts a large multi-national audience of well-paid business people. Your local bargain shopper newspaper probably focuses on working-class folks looking for inexpensive bargains. The daily newspaper tends to do best with homeowners. A mail order tabloid often goes to thousands of individuals interested in making money through the mail. Many of these readers live in small, rural towns. The Internet, by its very nature, appeals to up-scale, well-educated audiences that tend to be in their 20s and 40s.

Write a powerful headline. With classified ads, the headline makes or breaks the ad. Think about how you read a page of classifieds. You skim the first few words of each ad (often printed in bold type) to get a split-second idea of what the ad is about. Internet ads give you a subject line of four or more words. This means your headline has to get the prospect's attention and tell them what your ad is about. Pack as much key information as you can into just a few words. For example, if I were selling a computer, my headline would vary depending on the audience. For a general family audience I would write: COM-PUTER, POWERFUL, CHEAP. In three words I've told prospects what the item is, something about its quality and benefit (powerful), and a clue to the price of the product. If I were advertising the same computer on an Internet newsgroup used by computer enthusiasts, I would change the headline to reflect their more advanced understanding: 450, NEW, 56K Modem (a good deal at the time I'm writing this.)

Keep the body of your advertisement short. Guess what? Shorter ads cost less. Even if you can stretch out with a 50 or 100word ad, make your writing concise. There's no need to write in complete sentences in classified ads. Lay out the essential information on your product or service, show the prospect how it benefits them, and give your contact info. To write that same sentence in ad-blurb form: Essential information, incredible benefits, call now 555-1212. Here are some words that work best in classified ads: free, new, amazing, now, how to, and easy. Veteran copywriter Bob Bly adds: discover, method, plan, reveals, simple, advanced, and improved. I always try to use the word "you," often in all capitals *"You."*

More importantly, track your entertainment advertisements. You're throwing your money down the drain if you don't know which ads are working and which aren't. Key your ads when you can. Good classified advertisers always code their ads so they know which work and which publications pull the best. If respondents are writing to you to buy or get more information, include a "DEPT-A" in your address. The "A" is code for a specific ad in a certain publication. When prospects are responding by telephone, have your ad include an extension number for them to ask for. This clever tactic can be used to code your on-line classified ads. I create separate web pages to correspond with each advertisement I write. Then I count the number of visitors to each page to see which advertisements pulled the best. By using these three simple techniques in your classified advertisements, you'll reach more of your best prospects, sell more, and reduce the money you spend on classifieds.

Sonya's Sizzling Website Advertisements!

Have you ever built a good-looking web page, advertised it on the Internet and quite a few people came to visit—but no one stopped to purchase anything? Here are some simple ideas you can use now to get your website sales going. How many times have you landed on a website that looks promising, but you can't quite figure out what they're selling? Odd but true, many websites have a hard time telling you why they are there.

Tell the reader in very clear terms what you are selling. Make sure your *"what I'm selling"* message is the very first thing the reader sees. Many sites get carried away will cool looking graphics. They figure that you'll love the look so much you will be happy to click around for 10 minutes to find out what's being sold. Most people don't have that kind of time or patience. Remember that all readers come to your site asking, *"What's in this for me?"* Tell readers, right from the start, what they will get out of your site. List the benefits of reading further and buying from you. Tell readers who you are. Internet commerce is still brand spanking new and many people don't quite trust it yet. This is typical for a new media still in its early stages. Before anyone will spend a dime with you, they have to have some idea of whom they're doing business with. I'm often surprised at how many web site designers go for a cold corporate look that provides few hints of who is behind the site. That's okay for Coca Cola or American Airlines–those names are household words.

For most us, though, the reader wants to know who we are. Give the reader your name, your e-mail address (in a link they can click on to write you), your phone number, and–in most cases–a physical business address. Writer Kathy Matthew's recently wrote that no one in their right mind is going to send money to someone they don't know and can't get in touch with easily. She's absolutely right. I also feel it's a good idea to include your picture. It might be a picture of you working with others, your workshop, or your showroom. Here is an even better idea, use an online business card that I mentioned earlier.

Pictures communicate a lot of information and go a long way in putting Internet shoppers at ease.

Make sure it's easy for readers to find your order page, find your purchasing information, and can locate a number to call to order. If your website's main goal is to sell something, put your Order Information form in an easily seen link on every page. I like to make it as clear as possible: Give readers several different ways to buy—via an on-line order form, with a toll free phone number, or by writing a letter (I'm always surprised at the number of people who still prefer the old-fashioned method.) Most consumers will give you a credit card number, while many businesses would rather mail a check.

Include comments from satisfied customers. Before people do anything they look to see who else is doing it. It's human nature. Be sure to pepper your website with testimonials. They can be short–"*Paul's piano lesson video is fantastic and super easy to learn!*"—or you can go into more detail about the benefits the buyer got from your business. Your testimonials will be more believable if they include the customer's full name, business name, and city.

Promote your site. Because Internet commerce is new, it takes a lot more visitors through your site before you get a sale. Increase the number of visitors and you increase sales. Advertise in email newsletters (write me for a list), on newsgroups that accept ads, trade links with other sites like yours, get into a co-op banner arrangement, and build your own house mailing list by offering a free report or newsletter.

Finally, remember that the Internet is an information-based media. People go on-line to find good *free* information. Put some articles on your site that tells readers more about your field of specialty. If you're selling a long distance service, put up articles on how to deal with calls at work, how to get rid of unwanted calls, and new developments in telephone service. These articles don't need to be long. A few paragraphs often do fine for hurried readers. You can increase sales today by keeping these six simple points in mind when designing or updating your website.

Internet Post Card Advertising

Although direct mail is one of the great standards of advertising, it is not the cheapest advertising that will assist you in closely targeting your best prospective customers. It takes patience to send your ads to just the right people. Therefore, post card advertising might be the most important factor for getting you the results you need quickly and inexpensively. Post cards are shrink wrapped packages of advertisement. They let you reach hundreds of thousands of targeted prospects at a fraction of the normal cost of direct mail. Jeffrey Lant's long-running card deck program on *www. WorldProfit.com* goes to 100,000 opportunity seekers and small business people. You can get a one–line classified for $99. A 5.5" x 3.5" card costs $1,500 and generally pulls in 50 to 300 responses. If all this is a bit too pricey for your business, there are ways to piggy back with other card deck advertisers. This is extremely common in some decks, especially for website advertisers. Here's how to do it. Get on the mailing lists for several post cards. Look for cards that are going after the same prospects you want. Contact the advertiser to see if you can purchase one side of the card or a one or two-line ad (which can be as low as $90).

Getting Your Power Classified Advertisement

Ever notice a classified ad that appears over and over again, week after week? It is somebody's Perfect Classified Ad. It may not be a literary item of beauty, or even an ad that is very appealing—but for some reason it gets sales for its owner. Getting your Perfect Classified Ad will come easier if you follow a simple plan. Write your ad in complete sentences. Then cut out nonessential words to make your ad the required length. Start sentences with action words and use short phrases. While you are at it, write several versions of your classified ad. I usually try to knock out six at a time. Next, test your ads. Run them all on free ad sites, in e-zines, newspapers, or magazines. Be sure to include a code in your response info so you will know which ad produced the inquiry or sale. Once you find an ad that works well, leave it alone. Resist the temptation to tweak an ad that is already successful. Don't worry if you or your associates become bored with the ad. Your audience is not as close to the ad and is only assured by its repetition. Harness the promotion muscle your project deserves to get noticed.

How To Advertise Your Business or WebSite On Radio

Recent trends show radio is rapidly becoming the advertising method of choice for thousands of businesses and web sites. Radio lets you focus your ad dollars on specific groups of customers. You can zero in on important towns and cities. Radio also offers lower prices than other broadcast media. Radio has long been one of the best advertising choices for small businesses. Almost everyone listens to radio, with more than 500 million radios in the US alone. On average, people say they listen to radio at least two hours per day every day. Choosing the right stations.

Most medium-sized cities have one big newspaper, six TV stations, and dozens of radio stations. If a radio station puts out one-size-fits-all programming, they will wind up with very few listeners. Instead, stations specialize in entertaining specific age groups, lifestyles, and subject interests. Radio's ability to go after a very specific kind of listener is its greatest strength. More mass appeal media–like a newspaper that goes out to virtually everyone in town–can't give you this tight targeting. With radio, you don't waste ad budget sending your message to thousands of people who aren't likely to be interested in what you sell. It is important to advertise on a station that reaches your best group of customers. A pop or Top 40 station will mostly appeal to teenagers and 18 to 24 year-old women. Country stations usually pull in quite a bit of 25 to 54 year-old men. A classic rock station would also attract 25 to 54 year-old men. A news/talk station would specialize in an affluent audience over 55 years old.

Radio programmers first look at an audience that isn't being served, and then they create a format to appeal to that audience. Think like a radio programmer and you will immediately see which stations your best prospects and customers are listening to. You can get ratings information provided by Arbitron, the company that measures radio audiences. Advertising agencies have access to Arbitron ratings, as do most radio station advertising departments. You can also find radio ratings for different cities announced at *rronline.com,* the site for Radio and Records, the industry's trade publication. Arbitron gives you several different ways to look at the audience. If you are going after women 25-54 you can get ratings for women 18-34, 25-34, and so on. All this can become a bit confusing when you're talking to a radio sales representative. Their job is to sell ads by putting their station in the best light possible. Just about any station can show they are number one or two in at least one demographic, even though the age group may be quite narrow (the old joke among radio programmers is "even though we don't have very good ratings, we're number one in men 18-24 who have hair loss".) Next, I will go on to buying radio advertisements.

An account executive at the media buyer company of Interep says that radio stations have been selling many more advertisements lately and their rates have been going up. Contact the national sales office of Interep for your radio advertisement needs. Expect to pay more for Morning Drive times (5am to 10am) than for other less listened-to parts of the day. A few years ago you could get 60 second spots in Morning Drive for $20 in a great many cities. Now it isn't unusual to pay considerably more. WOR, New York City's famous news station, charges $200 to $600 per commercial. News station KRLD in Dallas charges $75 to $350 depending on what time of day you advertise, says Keli Carey of *RadioAirtime.com,* a site that helps businesses buy radio advertising nationwide.

Leslie Speidel, a veteran media buyer in Raleigh, North Carolina, says Morning Drive spots in her market are $400 on a top station and $100 on lesser-rated stations. *"I can usually lessen the pain for the advertiser by combining Morning Drive with lower priced commercials in other parts of the day,"* she says. This points out a fundamental aspect of buying radio. You get a much better deal by buying advertising packages. Stations will sell you multiple commercials at different times of the day to run over weeks or months. The price of individual spots can drop significantly. These days the radio industry is consolidating rapidly. It is not unusual for one large corporation to own hundreds of stations all over the country. It is not unusual for one owner to run five or six stations in your city. For example, Cathy Hughes an African American and owner of Radio One whose Lanham, Maryland headquarters office and two of her top radio stations (Magic 102.4 & WOL) are around the corner from my home has been doing quite nicely with several of her national radio stations. Her radio sales people can arrange for you to have your commercial running on several different stations with different formats and individual audiences.

How to Produce Your Radio Advertisement commercial

Most radio stations will produce your radio commercial for you at no additional charge. In most cases, the sales person who places your spots will also write your ad copy. It will be recorded by one of the station's DJ's (or "air personalities" as they like to be called.) Radio stations have to do a lot of work very quickly. Although some sales folks are excellent writers, most weren't training for that part of their job. You may do better to enlist the help of a professional writer. Contact local writing clubs. Search for freelance writers online.

Sixty-second ads are usually a better deal than 30-second ads. They only cost a few dollars more and double the time your message is on the air. Be sure to repeat your main benefit you offer customers at least three times in your commercial. End with your phone number, store address, or website URL so listeners can remember it. DJ's are often in a rush to get through the day's production chores. You can get better quality by insisting on meeting the air personality who will record your spot. DJ's have big egos (I used to be one) and really appreciate it when an advertiser shows them respect, gratitude, maybe even brings along a sample of their product as a gift.

Reaching out a hand can greatly improve the quality of your spot. Not many advertisers go through this little bit of trouble, but those who do get far better results. Live ads and on-location remotes. The most effective radio ads are often the ones that are read live by the DJ. The audience regards the air personality as a familiar friend and puts more confidence in your advertising message when the personality reads your spot live. Most DJ's don't keep an eye on the clock when they are reading a live ad. If you encourage the personality to ad-lib your spot in their own words, they will often spend more time on your commercial than your allotted 60 seconds. I've seen one-minute spots regularly go 90 seconds to two minutes.

When you buy an advertising package, see if you can get a live remote included. The radio station will appear at your place of business for one, two, even three or more hours with a personality promoting your store live on-air. Stations often bring attention-getters like brightly painted vans, huge inflatable mascots, and even free food for customers. Make sure you have plenty of staff on hand to convert visitors to buyers.

While we might figure that radio is an older media that may be getting left behind by the Internet, just the opposite is happening. The crush of web-based businesses have moved to radio to give them affordable, targeted advertising in specific markets. The great explosion of small businesses in the last few years is looking to radio to give them a promotional boost. Take time to consider using radio in your advertising mix. Articles are easy to write when you use this simple formula. I have given this formula to clients at my workshop and seminars. Everyone in the workshops is able to use it to write professional quality articles.

1. Start by pointing out a problem your reader has. I could have started this article: *"Spending lots of money on advertising and still not getting the results you want?"*

2. Then make your reader's problem seem worse. Point out the ways this problem can impact their business, life, and happiness. *"Your ads bring in only temporary response. Without an effective and affordable way to get the word out on your business, you may be closing your doors before the year is over."*

3. Next, suggest one to five ways the reader can solve the problem or make the situation better. *"One simple way to get lots of new prospects and customers is to write articles for trade publications in your industry."* I could go on to explain how to write an article (as I'm doing now).

4. End your article with a paragraph or two that reviews your most important points. Wrap up with a positive spin that paints a bright picture for your reader. *"Many entrepreneurs and professionals use their articles to launch successful national careers earning healthy six figure incomes. By following these easy steps, you can become a widely-respected exert in your field and give your business a big boost."*

5. Finally, include your contact info in a final paragraph at the end. Now that readers are impressed by your good ideas, they will want to contact you to pay for more information, services, or products. Many publications will allow you to include four to six lines that provide your contact information and even a plug your latest product or service. Most e-zines are like articles a page or two long (200 to 400 words). Magazines increasingly want articles that fill just one of their pages (900 words). Keep your sentences and paragraphs short. Avoid sentences that require several commas. The idea is to write in a style that is clear and easy-to-understand for a reader that is in a hurry. I think writing simply is also easier. How-to articles don't have to be fancy.

A friend often reminds me that I like to write, but most people, including her, hate to write. *"Everything you type looks wrong and an hour later you haven't gotten anywhere,"* she says. Many of us don't have time to write or don't feel it is one of our strengths. No problem. You can get a writer to do the work for you or hire an editor to polish the words you have written. A fellow writer who ghostwrites books for other people confided many well-known business writers don't do their own writing. Bill Gates has several good books, but professional writers wrote them all for him. He probably doesn't have time to sit down to write 200 pages.

Check with your local library for a list of writing clubs in your area. A quick look around my town turned up groups of non-fiction writers, technical writers, even a group of successful romance novelists. These are fertile sources of expert writers and editors, many who work for low prices. Also approach English teachers, journalists, do a search for writers on the Internet, and ask people who write articles you like. Give the writer the general idea for your article and some information to draw from. Then let them use their creativity and expertise to write the article.

E-zines are in constant need of fresh articles. Submission procedures are informal. Many welcome unsolicited articles. Simply e-mail the editor an article with a short personal note. You may find it best to first write the editor for permission to send your article. Gary Christensen has compiled a big list of editors looking for articles at: *www.site-city.com/members/e-zine*-master Kate Schultz's *EzineArticles.com* will distribute your article to a big list of editors.

Most magazines have specific submission rules they want you to follow. Some want you to pitch your article idea in advance via a query letter. Others invite writers to submit articles on certain topics that will be included in future issues. Check magazine websites for submission guidelines. Once an editor discovers you can supply them with good articles month after month, you can parlay your articles into a regular column. Now here comes the enthusiastic wrap-up: In a complicated world where every problem seems to require an expert, lots of new customers will respond to the useful information you provide. Write your own articles to make yourself an expert in your field. Don't miss your chance to tap into this powerful, no-cost form of marketing.

Did You See My Website…? How to Advertise for Free

When I first started advertising and marketing for Community TV USA Network, I had to first practice with using the free promotional and marketing tools offered by various website hosting services. The Internet was still brand new and a small organization does not have deep pockets of cash flow to do a lot of experimental marketing research.

Major search engines can be an incredible form of *free* advertising. Get your site listed high on a major search engine and your hits can zoom to 2,000 visitors a day. Sales will soar overnight! Unfortunately, you and many others will have a hard time getting that elusive search engine listing. You may have tweaked your site for what search engine spiders are looking for, then carefully registered your site with dozens of engines, and then waited weeks while nothing happened.

Let me give you some surprising reasons why your listing isn't getting seen. I'll also let you in on some ways to easily get in the back door of key search engines. Oh no bad new! they lost your listing. Last year Alta Vista, which had just bumped past Yahoo in popularity, suddenly dumped millions of listings from their database. Reports say they accidentally reformatted a few key hard drives. OOPS! If your hits started drooping, the Alta Vista problem could be the explanation. Meanwhile, several major search engines where taking your URL submission and would promise to index your site. We now know they were unceremoniously dumping those submissions in the trash. If you went back and tried to find your listing and it wasn't there, you probably were not listed.

And Yahoo is another story. While they attract a full 55% of search engine users, their directory is notoriously hard to get listed on. Be sure to check and re-check your listing. Take a moment to see if you are currently listed in major search engines. Expert Jerry West says there are really only three that you need to be concerned with. *"Type your web address into Yahoo, Alta Vista, and Excite. Those three account for 88% of all search engine traffic. If your site comes up, you're listed,"* West says. I checked to see if my website Swinton International Enterprises was listed. Because I registered with all of them last month, I figured I would pass with flying colors. I was dead wrong. Alta Vista had us listed fine, Excite didn't have us listed but offered me wallpaper with my domain printed on it, and Yahoo came up with a site that I discontinued a year ago (the old *swintonsociety.org* instead of the new *royal-swinton-society.org*). So I had to use my old egg-noggin brain. If you can't get through the front door then try the back door. And it worked.

You can easily get listed on several major search engines by going through the back door. Yahoo uses the Google database. Get listed on Yahoo by first getting listed on *Google.com*. Several other search engines, HotBot.com included, get their listings from the Inktomi database. Get listed on that database by submitting your site to *Canada.com*. (like doing business with the Canadians). I found some reasonably prized portal white window bars for my ground floor condo. The Canadian search engine will have you up in three days or less. By default, the others will have you listed, too.

Also hop over to *dmoz.org*. This is the Open Directory Project begun by several key players from Netscape. It's a snap to get listed and their database is the one Lycos and Hotbot use. By all means RE-register with Alta Vista—three or four times. Alta Vista has several databases they rotate (which explains why your site is listed high one minute and not the next). Submit your URL every week for four weeks to cover the entire system.

While you are at Alta Vista, check their short tutorial on how to write Meta Tags for your pages. Find it on the *add url* page Several engines use Meta Tags to list your site. Take time to write an appealing description for your site to go in your Meta Tags. This is the description that appears next to your link on search engines. Even if you aren't ranked tops, a good description will draw plenty of traffic. Make sure the words people use to search for you are listed in your title page and again in your page's copy. If a search word appears in the title but not the copy, the engine will ignore it. Keep up on the latest developments with search engines at *SearchEngineWatch.com*.

Chapter 3

Marketing On the Internet

That's My Website: "I'm A Proud Cyber Baby"!

Are you thinking of starting a small entertainment business, adding to the business you already have, or introducing a new product or service? Wouldn't it be nice to have a good idea of how successful you'll be selling over the Internet before you even start? That's the money making edge that smart market research can give you. You've probably heard that market research is expensive, only something that a bigger company can afford. That's partly true. Even a relatively modest research program can eat up several hundred thousand dollars in a hurry. But market research doesn't have to be so complicated only expensive consultants can figure it out. Here are some very simple ideas and tools for getting a pretty good idea of where you stand—*before* you shell out big bucks for marketing and advertising.

Internet Entertainment Market Research

It is worth reiterating again that selling most products and services over the Internet have a slim chance of success without a good, strong marketing program to promote products. No small business has the budget to do a saturation ad campaign that attempts to reach everyone. There's no need to. Your entertainment business, no matter what you're selling, most likely only needs to get the attention of a select group of good prospects. Internet market research techniques help you get the factual information you need about your target audience and pave the way for the effectiveness of your message. If you are wondering which new product to offer, Internet market research can poll people who have bought from you in the last six months, people who bought once but never bought again, and people who usually buy from your competitors. This will give you a very good idea of how well your new product will fare once it's introduced.

Research Samples That Work: The Secret of Getting a Good Marketing Sample

While Internet market research can be very complicated, there are a number of simple techniques that will deliver fairly reliable results. Quantitative market research methods provide statistical information. A carefully chosen scientific sample is studied as a representation of the larger public. In other words, 150 people are chosen. If we've chosen them with an eye to good sampling methods, those 150 will closely represent everyone else who is included in the target audience. This can be a bit trickier than it seems. You've surely seen the market research person with a clipboard standing in the mall asking people if they'd like to take a survey.

Several years ago, I was shopping at my neighborhood mall and a market researcher selected me, and several other mall shoppers, to participate in a random study of a lunchtime treat called *hot pockets*. Hot pockets are the microwaveable sandwich meals that have different varieties of meat wrapped up in a doughy outer covering. It was lunchtime and I hungrily jumped at the offer but first I had to go through a long list of questions before I could take one bite of the lunchtime treat. This was market research at its best. There was not a shortage of research participants; hungry mall shoppers like me were dying to eat anything and everything. Question? Would this be a good sample of the entire community? Sorry but I don't think so because not everyone goes to the mall. This sample would not work effectively because a great many people, including people who don't own cars, people who live a long way from the mall, and older folks who don't leave home often rarely or never go to the mall. Mall shoppers may be inordinately young, or more affluent than the rest of the population. It wouldn't be accurate to assume that mall shoppers represent the entire community. However, the market research person in the mall might get a very good picture of what the mall-shopping community is like.

The most common kind of quantitative research (the kind that provides you with numbers and percentages) is the telephone survey. According to Mark Bacon, author of *Do-It-Yourself-Marketing*, *"although this method can be fairly accurate, not everyone has a telephone and a great many people have unpublished numbers"*. This will reduce the accuracy of your findings, although you will still be way ahead of the mall survey.

Although market research performed at a mall isn't very good from a statistical standpoint, you can use this simple research to get ideas for new mass products and services. Just like some restaurant chains, give customers a short questionnaire to fill out. You could have them leave their comments for improvements of your new services. Try to give incentives if you can with a discount or free offer. Home-grown research, from entry forms on your counter to spending time on the phone with a prospect, can show you new ways to expand your successful products and services. Have you ever heard of the method of selling wide, selling deep to make more money?

The best solution for this method is to use a computer program that will give you a random list of telephone numbers in your area. These programs can be purchased, and most university communication departments have them for student use. Perhaps a student can print you a randomized list of telephone numbers. You can also mail surveys to entertainment corporations, or visit them in person, through this method. Sample locations of entertainment and media agencies can be researched by demographics. All of this will help keep subjective opinions out of the research.

You can do surveys with randomly chosen e-mail addresses provided those in the study have given their permission to be contacted. Most market research is based on simple statistics. No higher math is required. You can do just about everything with a simple calculator and advice from your Junior high school aged child. If you want further information about scientific sampling and the statistics you can perform on your sample results, please consult one of the great many books on market research. It's a subject that has remained largely unchanged for the past 50 years, so an old tattered volume in the used bookstore or at the public library will do just fine.

How to Make More Money Through Marketing

Here's one of the most durable marketing rules to use for the Internet, one that's been around for years. It's good advice for any business. If you want to sell lots of entertainment products and services, if you want to expand your business with loads of eager new customers—*"sell wide, sell deep"*. Let's look at this timeless rule of good marketing. It's full of ideas and inspiration that can fatten your pocketbook rather quickly. The best ideas are ones that help you work smarter, not harder. Here's how *"sell wide, sell deep"* works. *"Sell wide,"* means that you should offer lots of products or services that follow a basic theme (for example: all things offered by a photographer). *"Sell deep,"* means that you should try to find lots of good variations on a successful entertainment product or service.

Let's say you have one product or service that customer after customer is ready to plunk down money to buy. You start thinking *"If I had ten products just like that one I'd get rich."* If you were a photographer, you could offer school photographic specials for the preschool school student to the high school group. That's selling *"deep."* Now offer different kinds of school photos and related pictures like candid photos of the various sporting events. You could offer the yearbook staff choices of candid photos of activity shots in the field of football, basketball, baseball soccer, tennis and track & field events, and etc. That's an example of selling *"wide."*

Many businesses find a big increase in revenue when they introduce customers to a low-priced product, then step them up to increasingly more involved and expensive products or services. Customers are ready to spend more for more advanced services as they come to trust and rely on you. If you aren't able to provide extra products or services yourself, contract with others to provide them for you. Many website owners swear by their *"back page"* items. You can easily offer your customers lots of products and services supplied by others at very little cost to your own company. How Do You Find a Winner? I suggest that you, Go Wide and Deep. All businesses start out with some idea of what they want to sell. In the beginning you develop a few promising products and services and put them out there to gage the public's interest. Some products work, others don't, and sometimes you get a request out of left field that turns into your most important profit source.

For instance, when my friend, Steven, started his own business, he said that he thought that handing out marketing advice would be his bread and butter but before long, someone asked him to write a press release. It never occurred to Steve to be in the press release business, but as soon as he put *writes press releases* on his website, he started getting dozens of orders and presto, a new profit source. He expanded it into lots of customized variations of press releases to be sent via e-mail, releases for regular mail, releases intended for major magazines and newspapers, and releases intended for e-mail newsletters.

The product line soon went *wide and deep,* much to the delight of his clients who were looking for just the right service tailored to their needs. His advice was that he listened closely to what his customers and prospects were saying. He also added that when his customers talked about a problem that they had, he automatically began to think of it as a hint for another product or service he could offer to solve that problem. He says that the unexpected suggestions were his most important opportunities.

Did you know that this simple research method could give you a head start? You don't have to wait for customers and prospects to suggest new products and services. Ask them in clever ways that get them thinking for you. Was it as effective as it could have been? What problems are your customers having that you might be able to solve for them? Customers can often see things that people inside the business overlook.

Principles of Marketing Your Entertainment Business On-line

Are you planning to put your business on the Internet, but want to speed up the learning curve avoiding costly mistakes? Have you been on-line for a while and need some fresh ideas to jump-start your Internet profits? Before you get entangled in all the latest Internet gizmos and tricks, keep in mind that sound business starts with good, basic marketing. That's a rule that many on the Internet have lost sight of this year. One big business after another has hired expensive web design firms to build pages filled with state-of-the-art programming that can run only on the latest specially modified browsers. For the average consumer, many of those $20,000 website crash browsers, make little sense, and don't entice anyone to buy.

Start your on-line efforts with a good, basic lesson in smart marketing. Jay Conrad Levinson and Charles Rubin's now classic little book *Guerrilla Marketing Online Weapons* makes sure you understand the fundamental moneymaking rules of marketing. Levinson quickly shows you how to find a niche for your product or service, define your attack, build an identity, get a theme, and advertise wisely and consistently. The essential concepts of good marketing are timeless and there's never been a better time to review them. Getting back to marketing basics is your best bet for making a splash on the Internet.

Give your website a lift with William R. Stanek's *Increase Your Web Traffic In a Weekend*. From using free ads, newsgroups, and buying banners to how to impress search engines, Stanek is quick to read, easy to understand, and full of sharp ideas. He's also developed several websites where you can go to register your work with dozens of top search engines and link libraries. Got a week of vacation coming up? Take some time to read Dr. Jeffrey Lant's book *E-Mail El Dorado*. Lant always packs his books with how-to detail; so don't expect to skim through this book during a lunch hour. E-mail is currently the most effective, direct way to reach lots and lots of prospective customers. Lant shares his aggressive e-mail marketing technique: get the e-mail addresses of your customers and prospects (with their permission) and consistently hit them with good information and commercial offers. Lant covers how to develop sales letter templates for working with lots of e-mail fast, how to use listservs, how to write e-mail copy, how to start your own e-mail newsletter, and how to utilize e-mail in building a network marketing opportunity. Order the book direct from the author (617)547-6372.

For a good all-round guide to Internet business and marketing, get a copy of Jim Daniels' *Insider Internet Marketing (www.BizWeb2000.com)*. This has become the Boy Scout Handbook of Internet marketing information. Daniels has a lists of several places where you can get low-cost and free marketing tools on the Internet. You'll find yourself keeping this book right next to your computer. Computer equipment is likely to take the biggest bite out of your Internet entertainment business budget. There's no reason to spend thousands on the latest-greatest showroom hardware and software. *Cheapskate's Guide to Bargain Computing* by Bill Camarda is a real eye-opener to hundreds of ways of saving money on hardware and software. (Don't read this book if you just bought a new system.)

The rush to compete has encouraged software firms to offer their latest programs for big discounts or free. You just have to know where to look. Finally, the last book is really a whole class of good books. The Internet changes so fast that a traditional publisher can't keep up with the pace of new developments. By the time a book is on the shelves, its contents are a bit out of date. Some writers, like me have solved this problem by self-publishing. In this way you can keep the copyright and 90 percent of the royalties. You can also update pages at any time if you like. This is often the most comprehensive way for experienced

Internet marketers. It combines targeting, copywriting, and e-mail techniques with classic promotional methods that are just making it to the Internet. Remember that you don't have to read an entire book to get loads of useful insights and resources. Take a few minutes to *read into* a book. Scan the table of contents for the chapters that apply to your situation. Usually a writer will put his or her most important ideas in the first 40 pages and the last 10 pages of the book.

The Internet has gone mainstream and big time! You can't turn on your TV without seeing a commercial with a website address prominently featured right below the company's logo. When my local town hall in suburban Maryland displayed a banner announcing it's new website, I knew the web page had come of age. If you don't have a website to market your business to your community and the world, it's time to get one. Web space is offered free everywhere, and there are super-easy HTML editors that make designing a website just about as easy as typing a memo. Here are two quick and easy ways to get a good-looking website in less than a week (and that's if you take your time doing it!).

If you need to get your website up now, and you don't have time to deal with it yourself, get a web designer to build your first few pages. Keep the design simple and promise not to ask for many changes after the job is done. Many designers will knock out a professional looking starter site for a few hundred dollars. Then–when you have the time–you can add more pages to your site using the suggestions below.

Design your website yourself. Keep the concept simple and use timesaving aids developed especially for beginning web builders. First you need a place to put your site. There are oodles of free space offered by *www.tripod.com* and *www.geocities.com*. At the beginning, I used the *www.angelfire.com* web hosting for Community TV USA Network's pilot marketing program.

These services also provide beginner directions on how to design a site. Geocities provides its web building directions at several levels of difficulty (or maybe I should say *"simplicity"*)—start-up, basic, E-Z, and advanced. Tripod sends newbies directly to their Homepage Builder. They also provide you with places to get free graphics to spruce up your pages. If you are a member of AOL or Prodigy, those services provide both web space and excellent HTML editors free for your use. Even those who aren't AOL members can download a free copy of the highly acclaimed and super-easy to learn AOL 6.0 Hot Dog Junior.

In fact, if you're brand new to HTML editors, AOL Hot Dog, Jr. is your fastest way to a professional look (I had a pretty enjoyable time using AOL Hot Dog Junior to publish some of my family and friends' web pages). Common word processing and desktop publishing programs now offer web design features, too. I've seen nice looking sites turned out with World Perfect and Microsoft Publisher. For more complete HTML editors, look into Microsoft FrontPage, Adobe Page Mill, and Claris Home Page. Keep your website information packed and text intensive. Keep the graphics down to one or two per page. Many of the nifty websites you see are done by expensive web design experts who are often more concerned with impressing each other than communicating well to readers. There's no need to feel like you have to compete with whiz-bang sites of the week. As long as your site has good entertainment information or an exciting special offer, readers will appreciate it.

There are many on-line tutorials and books that can help you along the way. *Web Design for Dummies* puts HTML design in the easiest terms. For those in a real hurry, Lisa Schmeiser's *Web Design Template Sourcebook* provides you with a CD-ROM of web designs. Most are aimed at the corporate world including product brochure pages, guest books, and order forms.

Use a title and headline that describes what your page or site is about. Be very clear about what you sell and what benefits you can bring the buyer. Tell a reader who you are and why your company does what it does. Put your picture on your page to help people feel like they know you (earning trust on the Internet is always a concern). Websites are rapidly becoming an essential part of marketing.

As millions of people discover the Internet every few weeks, you will want your business represented by your own custom website.

Entertainment Marketing With Search Engines for a Profit

Have you had this experience? You go to your favorite search engine, type in a keyword for the kind of websites you're trying to find, and the search engines comes back with *"There are 20,132 pages that contain this information."* Yikes! Where do you start? The people who design search engines have heard your complaints. Most have been working hard to make search engines smarter. Here is how engines are changing and how you can take advantage of these evolving features. With the exception of Yahoo, which uses real people to review websites (and, technically, isn't really a search engine), all search engines are computers.

When you register your URL (website address), the computer runs over, takes a quick look through your site, and reports the information back to the search engine's data banks. In general, computers aren't as smart as people; so savvy web designers have come up with all sorts of tricks to talk search engine computers into giving them a high listing. No doubt you've clicked over to the top two or three listed sites, only to find that they have little to do with the topic you're searching for. That's exactly what search engine designers are trying to get away from. Increasingly, today's smarter engines look at the title of your site, the Meta information that you've included in the Head of your HTML code (we'll get to that), and the actual words that are on your page. If you put *"Washington Redskins Football"* in your title and Meta info, but your web page is about how to play an instrument, the search engine knows something is wrong. It won't give you a good listing.

All this means is that it's easier than ever for busy business folks to put together a website that search engines will like. Here's what to do: Make your web page (or your entire site) closely focused on a topic that can be summed up in a *single* keyword or two. My site is about *advertising and marketing*. The title of the page (the name that appears in the little box at the top of your browser), the Meta information, and the words on my page all talk about *advertising and marketing to the entertainment industry*. When a search engine indexes my site, the computer has no problem figuring out that my site really is about entertainment *advertising, marketing and promotions*. Different search engines focus on different aspects of your site, but most place a heavy emphasis on your title—that line in the box on your browser. Be sure to include your most important key word. Some people like to include it twice if they can use it in a logical sentence. I use content, *Advertising, Marketing and Promotion On the Internet to the Entertainment Industry*.

You can use this same code. Simply remove my title and put in yours. Then replace my keywords with ones that describe your page. Notice that I've used *marketing* several different ways. Keep it down to seven times at most (otherwise the search engine will disregard the keyword). Some search engine experts are now advising not to repeat a keyword in any form or fashion because engines are starting to penalize. Many top sites now simply list seven or so keywords and leave it at that.

Search engines can't yet read pictures (even the smartest computers still get human faces confused with pictures of pie!), so provide lots of information that talks about your main theme and keywords. In other words, make your site about what your title and Meta info claim it's about. All this makes it harder for web designers to trick search engines. In a way, that's good for those of us who are too busy doing other things to become experts in search engine registration. There's a simple formula for success: Design an entertainment website that is full of good information on a particular topic, and give the site a name that clearly and accurately describes it. That's good marketing, too!

Now, I know you're in a hurry, so you'll be pleased to know that 80% of the people using search engines go straight to one of the six biggest:

Alta Vista: www.altavista.com

Excite Search: www.excite.com

InfoSeek: www.infoseek.com

Lycos: www.lycos.com
Overture: www.overture.com (formerly www.goto.com
Yahoo: www.yahoo.com

Here's a tip…while Yahoo is hard to get listed on, they use the same database as *www.hotbot.com*.. That's right, get on Hot Bot and you will automatically be on Yahoo. Right now you can register with the first six with one click at *www.all4one.com.* Go to each engine and look for the link that says, *Add URL.* For Yahoo, you must first go to the listings of sites like yours, and look for the *"suggest a site"* link on that page. I also advise registering with AOL Netfind. AOL's 21 million members make it the single largest window to the Internet.

Granted, I've tried to explain search engine registration in simple terms. There are many more insights and nuances you can explore (a whole industry has grown up around search engine manipulation). But following these simple guidelines will ensure that your website is search engine-friendly. You will be much more likely to receive a favorable listing that will drive many more prospects to your website.

E-mail Marketing Strategy for Profit

Many types of Internet advertising don't work as well as they once did because people have gotten used to banners and don't click on them. Some e-zines have failed to keep their readers' interest and ads sometimes get less response. Search engines are over-flowing with submissions. Getting your site listed high is almost impossible, there-fore, more and more entertainment websites such as *atomfilms.com* and *reemind.com* (where I'm listed as a photographer) are now turning to e-mail marketing to keep profits rolling in. While an increasing number of people say they rarely surf the Internet, the vast majority of North Americans check their e-mail every day. I know I check my e-mails quite regularly throughout the day.

E-mail marketing is the most effective and efficient way to influence purchases and keep customers informed and happy. It is also extremely inexpensive. Where you might have mailed out one printed customer update every month, you can now e-mail one every week for a fraction of the cost. Increasingly, companies need to embrace e-mail marketing in a big way in order to stay competitive. Those who formerly used a service to send out their newsletters, sales info, and consumer updates are now doing all the e-mailing themselves. New technology that is powerful yet easy to use allows anyone to handle e-mail jobs that previously required expensive professional help. Many companies are bringing their e-mail campaigns in house in order to have more control, grow their e-mail efforts, and decrease costs. Here are four features you will want to use in your e-mail marketing efforts:

1. Include HTML in your e-mail messages. Most e-mail programs are now equipped to read HTML. Your logo, banner, bullets, and color elements can make your message jump off the screen. You can even include forms that allow customers to order instantly from your message. You take advantage of impulse purchases that can lead to big increases in sales.

2. Use a campaign manager feature to schedule when your e-mail messages will be sent out. You can prepare an entire month' worth of messages and tell the manager which weeks, days, or hours to release them to your list.

3. Take advantage of a POP import feature. It automatically takes the e-mail addresses from messages you receive and puts them on your mailing list. This insures no one who requests information from you is left out of your next update. This also helps you grow your list as fast as possible. You can even use a feature that automatically unsubscribes those who ask to be removed from your list. Many companies say this saves them hours of work each week.

4. Make sure the software you use to send your messages includes a walk-through wizard. You get step-by-step instructions on how to do any task you wish to achieve. Instead of waiting for the tech guy to show up, you can speed through the job on your own.

Smart Public Relations For Your
Small Entertainment Businesses

Sally Moore opened her favorite entertainment magazine to find a fawning interview with Military Entertainment Association's John Masson. Then she picked up the morning paper and read a long story on a new sports arena being built in her city. Did you know that the media hands out millions of dollars in free publicity every day? As effective as advertising is, a media story about you almost always pulls well. I have found that the familiar and respected voice of a newspaper editor, magazine writer, TV reporter, or radio personality talking about you holds lots of weight with the audience. For instance, when I got my first job working at the local government cable TV channel, I was selected primarily on the feature article written up about my cable TV program, *The Sonya Show*. This was a student-run production for my Howard University graduate internship program. Although, most of the candidates applying for the job were communication majors with television production backgrounds, I had very limited experience in television production at the time, but I had a lot of hands on experience in marketing and public relations. I suspect that the article written about my cable TV program set me apart from the others by establishing me as a little more knowledgeable.

How do all these businesses get media coverage? The secret varies depending on what your business does and how big it is. Large entertainment companies in-the-news like Disney Entertainment and Dream Works Film get coverage for practically any development. Political figures find their words in the media for almost any political debate. The local college football team gets press even if there is nothing much to cover. Your small business can have a much tougher time if you try to approach media the same way big organizations do. Media is almost entirely owned by large conglomerates and staffed by media pros who have never worked in a small business. The overall industry mindset is that big business is news and small business is–well–rarely news.

But this can all change to your advantage, if you offer good information or advice that will be helpful to the media outlet's audience. Newspapers love it when a tax expert offers tips around tax return time. Radio stations get a big kick out of anyone who can keep his or her audience laughing. TV likes anything that is visual and brings out emotion (hide the keys to a new car in a pool of Jell–O, ask contestants to swim to win, and watch every TV station in town turn out).

Let's focus on you as the media savvy expert. This is without question the best strategy for consistently getting your small business in the media. Start by taking inventory of the areas in which you are an expert, or hope to become an expert. Think in terms of the kinds of information a general audience would find interesting, helpful, or moving (these days many in the media try less to explain and more to create emotion). If you have a day care center, make a list of ten ways tired parents can keep an energetic youngster entertained.

If your area of expertise can relate to a hot topic in the news—that would be great! Historians, lawyers, detectives, and political scientists get in the media several times each year by giving informed tips relating to an event or scandal in the news. You may even be able to provide a local angle for a national story.

I have found the best way to get covered by newspapers is to first find the reporter who handles stories like yours. Most papers give reporters wide leeway in what stories they cover. Call the reporter and deliver a short, to-the-point message on why you have a story his or her *audience* would find interesting. Get to the juicy, memorable part first. Follow up quickly with a press release, question and answer page, and a bio about your business history (sometimes called a backgrounder).

While you have these materials in hand, call local talk and news radio shows. Speak with the host or producer. Explain what is interesting about your information and, again, follow up with your release, Q&A, and bio. The same strategy can work for getting you on top radio morning shows. Radio comprises well over half of all the media outlets in the United States and many other countries. Don't over look it. As you get media coverage, collect quotes from the media folks who have worked with you. *"Darrell Swinton kept the audience spell bound for over half an hour"* Little Rock, AR USA *"Interesting information every comedian beginner should know."* The Arkansas Gazette-Democrat, AR. Build your list of stations and publications that have featured your small business. Include reprints when possible. Media folks love to cover stories and feature experts who have already been successful elsewhere. Stay in touch with media who cover you. Send a handwritten thank you note to editors, reporters, and on-air personalities. Make sure you are seen as the expert they think of when your topic comes up in the news throughout the year.

Internet Marketing the Smart and Profitable Way

Recently, businesses have started tallying up what they spend to get each customer. One entertainment event coordinator estimated that for every new customer, it would cost at least $100 in advertising. An e-commerce firm figured out that by the time they advertised and gave away free things to get customers, the cost was $250 per customer. This illustrates one of the biggest problems entertainment businesses have. Generally, when we think of building bigger pro-fits, we think about getting more customers. That isn't the whole picture. For bigger, quicker profits, you should market to the customers you already have.

It would be great if your marketing hit the consumers and instantly persuaded them to buy from you now, but the process is almost always more complicated. Here's why focusing entirely on new customers can bleed your marketing budget dry with little sales to show for it. Before anyone buys from you, they have to step through at least four stages. The first stage is that you have to get the attention of the prospective client (the toughest stage of all since we are bombarded with hundreds of marketing messages every day). Secondly, you have to get the prospect to think about your offer. Thirdly, you must have the prospect make up his or her mind to buy from you. Lastly, but most importantly, the prospect must be motivated to take action to buy from you.

All four steps take marketing effort on your part. Each step can represent another advertisement you need to buy to march your prospects toward a sale. Even after someone buys from you, they may not come back to buy again. Studies show many people can't accurately remember where they bought things several weeks after the purchase. Meanwhile, current and past customers are the easiest to sell again. All this clearly leads to the need for you to stay in touch with customers you already have. Also include in this group hot prospects that have shown an interest in your business in the past. These are the most targeted and willing audiences you will ever find.

Start right now to make a list of people who have bought from you in the last week, during the past month, over the past six months, and within the past year. The idea is to develop different list so you can send just the right offer to interest and motivate them. If you clearly see that a big group buys one product or service while another group goes for a different offer, divide your customers up along these lines. You can double, triple, and quadruple your response rate by making your ads zero in on just what a customer or prospect is truly interested in buying.

Here's how this works. Lonetta's sewing shop includes two major groups of customers: people who buy supplies to make crafts and people who like to design and make their own clothes. Some of the crafters only come in around holidays. Others are more active during summer months when they spend more time out doors. A large group of those who design their own clothes have no interest in crafts.

Lonetta can develop specials, new products, and offers to deeply interest each of her main groups of customers. The seasonal crafters can get her mailed flyer one month before each major holiday and two months before Christmas. Others get her information monthly or only during winter months. You can use any database program to keep your lists organized. Most word processing programs include a basic database feature, or you can use a more specialized program like Microsoft Access.

The main reason for working your in-house list of customers and hot prospects is to keep your business in their minds. These days, people have numerous opportunities to spend their money , even when buying specialized products and services. If you live in a city of any size, there are anywhere from a few to dozens of businesses selling the same things you do. There may be thousands more on the Internet that can take your customer's credit card order and deliver the product within a few days.

If you don't work to stay in the minds of your customers, others will. But how do you work your list without taking out a major loan from the bank? Sticking stamps on thousands of letters can add up in a hurry. Smart marketers who have come before us have endured all the trial and error to give us two good answers. Thousands have found their best low-cost marketing tools for working an in-house list are postcards and e-mail. Postcards are cheaper than letters to send and don't require the customer to open an envelope.

Not having an envelope will be a big advantage. I didn't fully appreciate this until I watched my neighbor pull his mail out of the mailbox, walk over to his trash can, and start to drop letters in after only a momentary glance at the envelope. Put a color photo or graphic on one side of your postcard. The other side should have your main offer in a bold, black headline. Follow it with a deadline for the offer. Busy people may put off buying and soon forget about you. Your postcard offer will never be more powerful than it is right now when the customer has it in his hands.

Finally, be sure to briefly tell people how to buy from you. List your website, phone number, store location, and e-mail address. Building an e-mail list is even easier and almost free. Unlike a postcard, your e-mail messages can contain just as much information as you want them to. But, be careful how you gather addresses. Get a free list management service like *eGroups.com or Topica.com*. Both will give you a form to put on your website to gather e-mail addresses. You can also place a printed form in your office or store so that customers can request to get on your list. Make sure you keep the form they filled out in case there is ever a question.

E-mail messages tend to work best if they offer helpful information along with brief advertising messages. A friend of mind put short articles, with tips that her clients will appreciate, at the beginning of the message, then followed it with a short advertisement. There's an old saying that 80 percent of your business will come from 20 percent of your customers. Building your own in-house list and marketing it consistently will allow you to pull even more business from people who have already proven they like to buy from you.

Market Your Small Business On The Internet with Newsletters

If you're promoting your small entertainment business on the Internet, you aren't alone. The latest surveys show that small businesses outnumber larger firms on the Internet by a margin of four to one. Corporations are advertising on the Internet just like they do with other media: contact an Internet advertisement agency, buy banner ads, and watch results come in. That works fine if you've got thousands of dollars to spend each month on advertising. But what if you're going it alone and your advertising allowance has to come out of the grocery money? E-zines are the answer. E-zines (short for e-mail magazines or newsletters) are quick and cheap to produce and often go to huge numbers of eager subscribers. Publishers don't have to pay for postage or printing, and the savings are passed on to advertisers in the form of extremely low ad rates. For inexpensive Internet advertising, it's very hard to beat classified ads in e-zines.

As is the case everywhere on the Internet, your ad's first line is what makes or breaks it. Use the first line to announce your most important customer benefit. And don't forget the two most powerful words in advertising: "you" and "free." The sentence– "You can get my FREE report"—always gets big response. Sometimes e-zine ads bring disappointing results. If at first your ad doesn't succeed, try and try again. There's an old saying in marketing that the first ad never works. Advertising brings home the bacon when you smartly repeat your ad week after week. It takes time (sometimes as many as seven times) before your advertisement gets the prospect's attention.

Put Out Your Own Internet Entertainment Newsletter

A lot has been written lately about the importance of networking to build your small entertainment business. When marketing & network expert George Fraser, author of *Success Runs In Our Race* polled hundreds of successful entrepreneurs on what they attributed their growth to, most replied *"networking!"* I excitingly had the pleasure of meeting George at his friend, Les Brown's speaking seminar and I agree. Nothing helps you network like our own e-mail entertainment newsletter. Your ideas and expertise along with product news and tips from customers go out to everyone you know and do business with. It's also okay to include some ads for your company and associates. Readers don't seem to mind ads if they're packaged along with helpful articles. People on the Internet are usually in a hurry, so keep your e-zine short. One or two articles coupled with two or three short ads may be all your e-zine needs. Keep lines short enough to fit into an e-mail browser and put a hard return at the end of each line (to keep them from breaking up when e-mailed).

For starters, you can send your e-zine out with your favorite e-mail program (a good free one is Eudora Lite—*www.eudora.com*). Later, when your subscriber list grows, you may want to upgrade to a major demo provided, most likely, by the same company that provides your website space. Get subscribers by placing free ads on classified sites, ads in appropriate newsgroups, and announcing your new e-zine to firms that specialize in keeping track of various lists of subscribers.

Chapter 4

Promotions on the Internet

"Can You Hear Me—Yet"?

Making money on the Internet requires a great deal of promotion. The cost is so low that you can create a splash on the Web with no more than a contribution from the your piggy bank. This makes the Internet the perfect place to market your small entertainment business. Internet promotion is fun. Many entrepreneurs love to promote far more than they like the day-to-day tasks of running a home business. Some jump from one new idea to another just so they can devise new promotional campaigns.

The Internet's most successful small business owners take a Barnum and Bailey approach to marketing, having a field day with the Internet's big selection of free and low-cost promotional tools. One person with online savvy can do the work of 10 people and spend almost nothing in making his or her name a household word. Marketing expert Jay Conrad Levinson has adapted his Guerilla Marketing approach to the Internet. His creative techniques are a perfect match for the Internet's do-it-yourself environment. Levinson's book *Guerilla Marketing Online* details a variety of ways you can professionally promote your site for next to no money.

Place your advertisement on the Web's thousands of free classified ad sites. Type *free classified* into any search engine for a complete list.

There are several free and low-cost programs that help you automate some or the entire task of posting your advertisements. Banner ad advertising is one of the top ways corporate web sites promote themselves. There are now many low-cost packages available for small businesses. Packages are either priced on a per *click-through* basis or on a *per impression* model. Per click-through buys guarantee you will get a set number of people to click on your banner and go to your website. Buy e-zine ads. E-zines, or e-mail newsletters, are the Internet's most affordable advertising media options. They pack a lot of power for very little money. Depending on the publication, ads are typically 3 lines to 50 words, costing between $20 and $40. Many reach 40,000 to 300,000 people. Even a small circulation e-zine can pull good results if it is targeted directly at your *best* customers.

Start your own e-mail newsletter. Nothing creates sales like your own Internet community. A big group of people who know your name, like you, see you as a person with good information, and hear from you often will provide a lasting, steady source of sales and revenue. E-mail newsletters are by far the best way to build your Internet community.

They are easy to produce and are almost free to send. Understand that most readers are busy, so keep your newsletter short. You can design your newsletter in any word processor. Keep lines about 65 characters long with a hard carriage return at the end of each line (hit enter). This will keep your lines from breaking up in your subscriber's e-mail reader. Get subscribers by putting a sign-up form on each page of your website. Also list your newsletter on all your correspondence and printed materials. The vast majority of e-zines are free to subscribers. Earn revenue by offering to run ads for your subscribers and other businesses.

Charging ten dollars per 1,000 subscribers is one way to price your advertisements. You can also list your newsletter ad offer in a growing number of e-zine directories. Swap ads with other e-zine publishers. You will get a lot further on the Internet if you are constantly looking for ways to join efforts with other entrepreneurs. Many small businesses have built large subscriber bases for their e-zines by trading ads with other newsletters. Simply send a note to other publishers saying you will run their 3-line ad in your newsletter if they will run your ad.

Through all your efforts to build your e-zine, you will be collecting subscribers. This *opt-in* e-mail list is the most powerful marketing asset you have. Never miss an opportunity to ask someone if they want to receive your information periodically. Add them to your growing list. Send out announcements of new products, lower prices, or new affiliations with other firms. Your e-mail offers should contain links to pages on your website that will give serious prospects all the additional information they want. Most e-mail programs now turn any address with http: in front of it into a live, clickable link. Use opt-in e-mail. This involves using commercial lists of people who have asked to receive messages about a particular topic. Suppliers of opt-in e-mail sell lists of people wanting e-mail on everything from business opportunities, to cars, to tax tips. You can send an e-mail message to several hundred people for as low as $40. Opt-in e-mail can often generate a success rate up to 17%, which is very high for direct marketing.

Don't spam. Sending out e-mails to people you don't know is called spamming. It is very unpopular with Internet users with some aspects being illegal in some states. Spamming is very bad for business and can create lots of problems including the cancellation of your Internet connection.

Promoting Your Website In Internet Malls

Get visibility in Internet Malls. These are large groupings of websites covering particular topics or product categories. There are Internet malls for business opportunities, for crafters, and for businesses located in specific geographical areas. People interested in your kind of products and services can find you in these handy one-stop-shop locations. A good mall can help you get your Internet business started with expert advice and easy-to-use credit card transactions for your customers. You don't have to spend big money, learn complicated programming, or hire more people to do handle the details. An Internet mall should receive plenty of promotion from its owners. Like anything else on the Internet, a mall needs to be aggressively marketed to get visitors.

How to Promote Your Business With Low-Cost Events and Clever Stunts

IPrint sends actors dressed as ancient Roman soldiers into downtown San Francisco to get attention and hype the company's latest offer. Evite's CEO wanders the financial district handing out thousands of brightly colored pens emblazoned with the company logo. The latest marketing trend in Silicon Valley is a time-honored guerrilla marketing promotion method that is almost free. Some of the Internet's hottest start-ups are pushing their products and ideas with promotional events, creative promotional stunts, and clever gimmicks.

Companies like Evite, Ask Jeeves, and *TheStreet.com* have made stunts, ranging from flooding Wall Street with singers to dropping fruit on passersby, an important part of their marketing plans. Why use this method that some might consider the poor cousin of mainstream advertising? Stunts and gimmicks work, especially when they are creative and well done. It wasn't too long ago that corporate web start-ups were awash in money. The conventional wisdom was you couldn't launch a new idea without a minimum of $20 million in advertisement and promotion budget. The tech crash that followed forced a lot of companies to abandon their lavish advertising. Instead, they are turning to the mother of invention, creativity. When you don't have cash, you get creative. This usually results in better, more interesting marketing.

In an age when all your prospects and customers are constantly bombarded by advertising, a good stunt can look unusual, get attention, and help your message cut through marketing and promotion clutter. Stunts often get media coverage. You come off looking creative and energetic in front of thousands of prospects. Once you have a great stunt in place, it doesn't take much copy writing to get television, newspapers, and magazines to cover you. Television is looking for something visual. Newspapers generally want an event that relates to a topic in the news. Create a team to solve a pressing local problem. Provide a humorous twist on a popular controversy. Call the news desk and ask who covers your kind of story. Give the reporter a quick rundown of the most interesting facts about your event (be sure to give them the juicy stuff first). Then follow up with a press release. Include your phone number and e-mail so the reporter can quickly get back to you with questions.

Free Publicity and How To Write Your Own Articles

Here's a simple method for tapping into an outstanding source of *free* publicity for your business. Everyone likes to buy from an expert. Shopping for a computer? A sales person who knows computers inside and out makes us feel confident about his or her recommendations. Planning to buy stocks? You would likely look for a broker who has Wall Street down pat. Here is an effective way to make yourself one of the leading experts in your industry. Write your own how-to-articles. Prospects and clients will read your articles, appreciate the good information you have to share, and look to you as an expert who can help them.

You don't have to be the next great novelist. Simply write a page of instructions that tells someone else how to do something. It can be information you learned on the job or advice you picked up in books and conversations. Customers buy because they have a problem that needs to be solved. When you appear as a helpful expert with lots of answers, you're halfway to a sale. Newspapers, magazines, e-zines, and industry newsletters all need a steady stream of good informative articles. It is easier to get your articles into smaller publications that closely target your best customers. Often these smaller e-zines and newsletters draw better response than some of the big glossy national magazines. If you are sending companies the information in advance of the date you would like it reported, write: FOR RELEASE: Friday, July 1 (for example). A word to the wise:

Don't expect them to wait if the news is really big. In fact, giving reporters earthshaking news in advance, then telling them not to report it for a few days, is likely to irritate them. Drop down a few spaces underneath the release date and type in all capitals a headline summarizing your message. Put your newsworthy information first. Lead with whatever you think the reporter will be most interested in. Let the less important details bring up the rear. Don't write your release like a feature story, beginning with something like, *"It was a dark and stormy night and Bill Gates woke up from his dream feeling vindicated from his Microsoft Antitrust ordeal."* Even though there seems to be a growing number of papers across the country that turn all their news into feature stories, it is bad journalism.

Keep your release to a page or two. Even a half-page release will often do the job. Reporters want the information quickly and with a minimum of effort. They will call you for more details, and these will frequently be details you never thought about including. Conclude your release with the sign "#" or "-30-" placed in the center of the page, immediately following your text. These are traditional ways of signifying that the release is finished. Keep your writing clear. Uncommon terms will require a quick explanation of what they mean. If the reporter may be unfamiliar with your point, compare it with something they'll probably know.

You can reinforce a concept by saying the same thing again in different words. This is valuable when talking with reporters. I learned this familiar technique when I was a photographer in the United States Marine Corps. I would travel along with the journalist of the Quantico Sentry Newspaper in Virginia and she would rewrite her story at least a dozen different ways. We covered award ceremonies and the entertainment and sports events on the military installation. Accentuate the important points of your message, saying them slowly so that the reporter can get them down.

The reporter is often writing the story as he or she talks to you. Listen and you will hear the clacking of computer keys as you talk. Some reporters say they appreciate a few handwritten words of thanks along with the news release. I know my reporter friend, Sharon (Tutt) Baker, always enjoyed receiving uplifting letters from happy interviewees at the end of a long day. Others say they are much more likely to open envelopes that have been addressed by hand. This may be particularly appropriate if you are trying to cultivate a personal relationship with the reporter.

When to Issue a Press Release

Watch for those opportunities when a news release will be appropriate and likely to get into print. I know my friends in my small town of Prince Georges County, Maryland always seemed amazed at how I got my little community pageants and fashion shows in the news along side the feature stories. It helps to always have a photographer present to take pictures of your event just in case the newspaper reporter will not be available to cover your story.

Try submitting official announcements, such things as appointments, new services, and organizational accomplishments, which are regarded as newsworthy. For example, writing about celebrities and public figures that are doing things with you and your organization is an excellent way to get free publicity (events such as Community Service events, open houses, tours, award ceremonies, accomplishments, anniversaries, rallies, and debates).

Public appearances and big media coverage can interest a reporter. If your work is being featured on *The ABC News*, let the newspaper's television editor know about it. Remember to watch for things you can tie in. Can you associate yourself with upcoming holidays, public service projects, and news happenings that are getting lots of attention? Watch for regular newspaper columns that deal with your area of interest. Journalists are especially likely to use your news release, sometimes in its entirety, if your message directly relates to the column's topic. If the paper includes a weekly profile of what's happening on radio, be sure to send them a release anytime you have a scheduled radio interview or when you have recently appeared on the radio with something interesting.

Remember to use the smaller local newspapers, newsletters, and the Internet e-zines! Often times when the big daily paper in your town isn't interested in your story (for example it has too much to do with your business interests with not enough interest for a general audience), consider a more specialized publication. For example, my mom, Lonetta, had a photographer take a picture of me for winning a first place local art award. She intentionally had it placed in the small but well read African American local community newspaper instead of the larger Arkansas Democrat-Gazette newspaper. Boy! Was I a celebrity for a week? My schoolmates' parents were really impressed.

Entertainment trade or industry papers and magazines can be excellent for this. The fact that you added a new CD at your Recording Studio is probably of no interest to the big daily paper. However, it might be a good story, accompanied with a photo, for a magazine, newspaper, or newsletter that specializes in musical recordings. If your business coincides with a minority group or opinion, look for publications, which target that smaller group.

There's nothing wrong with reaching a smaller audience, especially if that audience is made up of a high percentage of your target prospects. One of the biggest problems with big mass media (like newspapers and TV) is that they send your message out to just about everybody. It's rare that a business actually needs everybody. Chances are that you will only need to sell to specific groups with certain types of interests and needs.

Tips From a Newspaper Editor

I recently spoke with a newspaper editor about what kinds of stories they would cover. Much of what she said is a repeat of the things you have read above. But she had several other interesting points that you would do well to keep in mind. Don't call the morning paper's office at 3 p.m. because it is deadline *crunch time* and no one will have time to take on a new story. The reporters and editors will be tired and stressed by this time. You will need to call earlier in the day when things are more relaxed.

Try to be concise and prepared to tell the reporter why this story is important to their readers, and don't ramble on with too many details. Get to the meat of what interests the newspaper. If you want the paper to publicize an event, get it in writing and make sure the paper has it one week in advance. Remember, your story has to be timely. If it happened last year, or even last month, it may no longer be of interest to the newspaper. News must be new.

Where Do You Find the Addresses for the Media?

It used to be that you had to shuck out a few hundred bucks to buy a media guide on CD-ROM. Now that just about every media entity in the world is on-line, the process of getting accurate addresses is much easier and cheaper. Gebbie, a well-known guide, has jumped ahead of the pack and put its addresses and links on a well organized website (*www.gebbie.com*). I recently sent a press release via e-mail to over 1000 of the radio stations Gebbie has listed and got very good results. Remember, bulk mailing your press release to media is not the same as spamming individuals. Media expects to get unsolicited promotional announcements. That's the business they're in. No media person in his or her right mind will object to getting your press release unsolicited.

There are also companies that will send your press release out for you, although I'm not so sure it's better than the do-it-yourself method. The top press release agency in the corporate world is PR Newswire, *www.prnewswire.com* and *www.newstarget.com*. This agency has cultivated a relationship with thousands of editors covering a variety of industries. I would take that with a grain of salt. A colleague of mine said that when he worked in media, they would often get calls or cards from PR firms asking if they wanted to get their press releases. He said that they would usually say, "yes" because they would sometimes send free hats, shirts, and other trinkets. "Too bad, the press releases often went into the trash," he said. It's much better if you cultivate your own relationship with editors. Also check out Automated Press Releases: *www.gapent.com/pr.*

For the nice price of $12.50 per hundred, they'll send your release to any of their 7,600 media sources in 37 countries. While you're at the automated site, read through their *Pet Peeves of the Media* article. Other great services are at www.usanews.net (*USANews.net*) *www.xpress-press.com pressPress.com.* Some PR firms will write your press release for you. The price usually runs around $200—$300 for a one-pager. Now and again somebody will say, *"tell me the absolute best way to get my press release used by the media."* There's no better way to get free media than to take the time to find exactly the right TV, newspapers, radio (etc.) to send your release to, and send it yourself.

Here's my advice. Get a copy of the Gebbie All-in-One Media Directory. Gebbie Press publishes the All-In-One Media Directory, list-ing: 23,000 USA TV/Radio stations, Daily/Weekly newspapers, Trade/Consumer magazines, Black/Hispanic media, syndicates, net-works and more. It is sold in print, on disk and on mailing labels. They've been doing this for 40 years and are the best around. For the price of paying a service to send your release out just once, you can get the famous Gebbie Guide and send releases over and over again to just the right media you chose yourself.

Important Promotions Tips

While news releases are not always effective for radio or television, they are an important part of newspaper operations. Get the name of the reporter covering your type of story and send your press release prepared in the standard format. Conventional appearance will tell the reporter that you are a fellow professional. Write clearly and make sure your facts are accurate. Include names and numbers for contact people who can be reached at any time. Reporters will often call back for further details or clarification.

Increase your frequency of media exposure by striving to be a professional and reliable source that the reporter will want to work with again in the future. Although there is no rigid standard for media releases, here is an example that will be acceptable to virtually everyone (excluding the content, of course). Here's a simple example of what a standard press release looks like:

Example of a Press Release to for the Media

L'Enfant Plaza
Washington, DC USA
phone: (202) XXX-XXX
Contact: Sonya Swinton
FOR IMMEDIATE RELEASE
ENTERTAINMENT VIRTUAL OFFICE
OUT OF THIS WORLD.

Swinton International Enterprises virtual office is out of this world—*virtually*! Technology website development agency offers a better way for new & small entertainment business owners on line to develop their website with their *virtual* state of the art office decor. For new small entertainment businesses will have a lot less to be worried about this year because a new international entertainment virtual office technology agency with teleconference capacity has come to the nation's capital.

How to Use E-mail strategies To Get Thousands in Free Media Publicity.

Never before has there been so much media. Internet, cable, satellite, new Community, Government & Public assess low power TV, and streaming media add to the already staggering number of radio stations, newspapers, and magazines. Competition is intense. Each year there is more pressure on editors and producers to find fresh stories and interesting information to satisfy their audiences. This is good news for you. If you have expert tips to share, an interesting new product or service to announce, or even a controversial opinion, many in the media will spread your news to their listeners, readers, and viewers. You get free publicity money can't buy when you help media folks get the fresh content they constantly need. Editors are often swamped with press releases bag loads arrive by mail, spill out of the fax machine, and fill up their e-mail. Use these strategies to get noticed and get your press release used. Because e-mail is instantaneous, try to constantly scan the headlines for a popular story or topic that you can relate your business to, and get your release to editors *ASAP* while the topic is still hot. Right after an important story breaks, media looks for related stories to keep the topic in front of their audiences. You can e-mail press releases to media inexpensively using a good media contact guide or database. We've had luck using the fine media guide at *gebbie.com* and the press release program available from *mediamagnet.com*. Most guides divide media into a number of categories: radio, TV, daily newspapers, weekly newspapers, and magazines.

Target general interest media. It's important to send your release to the kind of media that will be interested in it. It's safe to send just about any release to the general interest media: film, music, radio, TV, newspapers, and general business and news magazines. Sending your release to everyone on the list will fill your mailbox with angry replies from editors. Once we got a stern reply from the editor of *Soil and Conservation Monthly* after we accidentally sent him a release of a local Community TV USA Pageant announcement.

Make sure to write your release to appeal to radio. The vast majority of major media outlets in North America are radio stations. Most cities have one or two major newspapers and a handful of TV stations, but they often have 15 to 30 radio stations. Radio overwhelmingly uses locally produced programming that has to be produced daily every day of the year. Since most radio stations are designed to entertain, they gobble up any story that is funny, sad, thought provoking, or pertain to a fashionable topic. Be sure to include your telephone number and offer to be available to do a live on-air interview.

Write a press release filled with your expert tips. It's okay for it to be a bit of a how-to article. Editors will use it if the information is helpful to people in their audience. If you are an accountant, announce a free checklist available to small businesses. Include your free tips in the press release. A web designer can provide ideas on how to make an entertainment business' website sell. When I used to be a children's performing arts director for the Children's Cable TV Workshop, I used to give parents and teachers some ideas on how to keep children entertained.

You will also want to choose some addresses from a list of magazines and newsletters that relate closely to your industry. Often these industry publications are easiest to get into and will give your business a greater amount of publicity. Things that seem like no big deal to a daily newspaper can be big news to a magazine or newsletter in your industry. Watch for the same email addresses to show up multiple times on directory lists. If you're not careful, you can end up sending two, four or even eight copies of your release to the same media person. Media companies often have one person who collects press releases for several stations or publications that operate within the same company or building. A single person can be listed as the contact for two to eight media outlets.

You can avoid the multiple-copies problem by alphabetizing your e-mail list. It's easy to spot duplicates of the same address. I found that out the hard way, when I had my press assistant send out information on my family's Royal Swinton Society. In America, royalty like our United Kingdom counterparts does not enlighten some people. It would be considered an offensive jester in Great Britain but in America, needless to say, there is no such thing as an official title of royalty or monarchy in the United States. Anyone can have the title of king, queen, lord, and etc.

In a media world that is increasingly dominated by mega-corporations, some media people think that one and two persons businesses are insignificant. I would argue that America's rich selection of media is only possible because of the First Amendment, which allows a free press and freedom of speech. It is your freedom to express ideas to media that guarantees the existence of media. It's also important not to abuse this freedom. Use your access to media wisely.

Two Top Ways to Promote with A Multiple Auto responders

A business colleague of mine says that, *"Your advertising is wasted if you don't follow-up on your leads."* Her solution is to use a multiple auto responder that sends her prospects a new sales message every few days. People need to see your ad message several times before they buy. Those who buy on the first ad have already made up their minds after seeing someone else's promotion. Yours had the good fortune of reaching the customer at just the right time. You can greatly increase sales with a three letter multiple auto responder. There are a number of places to get these auto responders free (*fastfacts.net, getresponse.com, smartbot-pro.net, xsponder.com*) and others who sell up-graded service at low cost. Make your first letter briefly present your offer. It should be designed to get attention and bring in those who tend to quickly make up their minds to buy.

Your second sales letter should arrive the next day. Make it longer and filled with details. About 70 percent of consumers are folks who need all the details before they will purchase. List your features and connect them with the benefit your customer will get from those features. Your third sales letter should be scheduled to arrive several days later. Start with *"Successful people are busy. I know you probably saw my earlier messages, considered them, but haven't yet had time to respond."*

Then give them another rundown on your offer. Bring in a fresh angle so it doesn't seem like they are reading the same letter they saw a few days ago. More than three sales letters tend to get ignored. If you want to send more, have your fourth and fifth letters arrive weeks or months later. Scheduling a new letter to arrive every month can catch a prospect when they're ready to buy.

1. Pick a problem that lots of your customers struggle with. In our business the big stumpers are getting a site that sells, finding a way to handle e-mail, figuring out search engines, and assisting clients with low-cost ways to advertise effectively. A course on any of these is guaranteed to bring lots of interested prospects and customers. Your course could be on how to complete a basement, how to avoid an IRS audit, how to give your kids straight teeth, or anything else that customers often ask about.

2. If you don't write or have time to pen your own articles, look for others who have written on the topic. It is perfectly legal to put their ideas in your own words (always proper to give them credit). You can also quote the article. It is best to ask in advance, if your course is for commercial purposes. Start your article and then say expert Blank and Blank has some valuable information. Include a few paragraphs of what Jane wrote. Be careful not to use so much you give away her entire article and spoil her ability to sell the information.

How To Use Your Free Link Pages To Promote

There are thousands of free link pages and millions of people use them. You can bet that they're crowded. But free for all link pages can be a powerful tool in the hands of anyone who knows how to use them with determination and flair. The Internet is the great free enterprise marketplace of our day. Like your great-grandfather began his business by placing his apple box near Times Square, you can use free for all links to shout your message at no cost or low cost in the big world of e-commerce. *Free for all link* sites feature a line of advertising with a link to your web page. Prospects can quickly and easily scan down a page of links to find products, services, and opportunities that interest them. Like a new service scrolling the day's headlines, free for all link pages give you a running update on what is happening on the Internet's front lines. Lots of people check them regularly to stay on the cutting edge.

Thousands of beginning (and experienced) Internet entrepreneurs have discovered free for all links are a great way to launch a new product, test an innovative service, or give their web site a quick boost of traffic. Here are four ways to make these free link opportunities work for you. For instance, try to use one of the services that blast your link to hundreds of pages. Even though lots of other people are doing the same, the number of visitors to these sites creates a collective crowd of potential customers. Services that charge a small subscription fee for access to their network can give you a less crowded field for promoting your link. Nir Leibovich, CEO of Linkomatic *(www.linkomatic.com)* points to recent improvements for free for all link enthusiasts. *"We have a proprietary license to over 3500 of these link pages and no one else can submit to them,"* Leibovich said. This means members of Linkomatic's network have their links stay up on link pages longer with more exposure.

Secondly, make sure that your line of entertainment advertisements copy sizzles. Start with an action word. Use marketing's two most powerful words: *free* and *you*. Offer your reader a benefit for clicking. Tell them what they will get when they arrive at your site. It may take some practice to get your message to fit into a single line. Readers should click your link to find a web page that exactly echoes what your line of link advertising said. Don't confuse prospects by promising them one thing in the link ad and hitting them with something different on your web page.

Consider getting your own free for all links page. You can harvest the e-mail addresses of those that place ads and send them your own marketing message. Because others voluntarily place their links on your site, you have a legitimate and valuable opt-in list to promote your services. Keep in mind that almost everyone who places a link is launching or promoting a small business. They will all need services, products, and ideas you can sell them. Try to focus your offerings on things that help them do their work faster, increase their sales, or can find them a viable opportunity.

When you place your link on someone else's site, expect to get an e-mail confirmation from them. It may be a good strategy to create a special mailbox or e-mail account just for replies. It will help you keep your free for all link promotion program organized. Be persistent. Your great-grandfather didn't get a free ride. He had to brave cold weather, rude people, and meager earnings. Eventually his persistence paid off. He built a business that grew each year and benefited generations of family with a solid income and a promising future.

Write your dream down on a piece of paper. List three to five steps that will get you to your goal. Put the paper in your pocket. Take it out several times each day and read it. Keep doing it until the paper becomes dirty and ragged. It can be responsible for vast fortunes. Constantly review your goals and the methods you will use to obtain them. This is vital for keeping you focused. It is an important step toward making free Internet promotion your path to a bright future.

Sonya's Super Duba-Search Engine Promotion

New techniques can drive thousands of visitors to your web site. My colleague Jennifer is the first to tell you that driving traffic to your website is an expensive proposition. *"I spent the promotion budget on ads, the grocery money on banners, and we still aren't getting that many hits,"* she says. Now Jennifer turns to search engines. She's heard that tens of millions use them each day to navigate around the Internet. A good listing on a major search engine can bring thousands of already targeted customers to her site. But how can she get her site listed-and fast?

As search engines get more sophisticated, it's easier to get a good site listed. It's also harder to *trick* search engines into listing you. The good news is, if you have a site that is focused on just a few topics that your best prospects are likely to search for, you're in a situation where the mammoth Internet portals can help you, and it's all free! Forget about those services that promise to list you on thousands of search engines. There are only three search engines that really count. Because a number of the majors use the same database, you can register on one and show up on several of them. *"Don't waste time trying to get on*

Yahoo," says Jerry West, search engine expert with NetGateway. *"Instead, submit your site to HotBot.com."* because both use the *Inktomi.com* database. A listing on HotBot virtually guarantees a showing on Yahoo.

Recently AltaVista surged in user popularity. It ranks as one of the best places to have your site listed. *Alta Vista.com* rotates visitors through four databases. If you don't see your site listed, try again in 15 minutes when the next database will be on display. Register with Alta Vista weekly to get your site listed in all four databases. You will also want to submit your web address to Excite, perennially one of the most used engines. Like HotBot and Alta Vista, Excite spiders through your site in a matter of seconds. Your listing can show up within a few days.

Search engines pay close attention to the title of your site. That's the line that appears in the little box on your browser. Take care to include two or three keywords that your best prospects are likely to type into a search engine when they are looking for a site like yours. *"Welcome to Joan Ellis' Website"* may sound good, but it doesn't give search engines much to go on. My friend Joan is a bank trust officer, and it would probably be better to title Joan's opening page with some words about what she offers, like *"Solutions for Veteran's benefits and debt expert, loan restructuring, and bankruptcy referrals."* That gives a search engine several good keywords to use when categorizing Joan's site, words that her customers are likely to use when looking for her.

Big companies now have access to records from all the major search engines. These databases can show which keywords people use for searching. Often a company can find a keyword that millions of people search with, but which isn't used by many websites. Using a popular but neglected keyword can draw a goldmine of new visitors. West says you don't have to give away big bucks for the insider's list of keywords. Anyone can find them by checking *www.Goto.com (now called www Overture.com).* The engine lists keywords that people use along with a rating of their popularity.

More and more, getting a good listing on search engines has less to do with tricks of the trade and more to do with how well your site covers a particular topic. After all, that's what people hope to find when they use a search engine. Spend time crafting an inviting description of your site to include in your Meta Tags (for a quick lesson on how to write your own Meta Tags, see Alta Vista's short tutorial at *www.altavista.com*).

Search engines display your description next to the link to your site. A good description can grab attention and cause lots of people to click to your site rather than another one. Be patient and don't get too obsessive. I find that once sites are listed on the six or seven major search engines, they tend to start showing up on many other search engines and link libraries. You can register your site with all the majors with one click at *www.all4one.com*. You can register free with over 400 search engines and link libraries *submit4free.com*. Finally, make sure the copy on your website is interesting and makes customers want to buy. All the traffic in the world won't earn you a dime unless your website converts visitors into buyers.

Making a Good Promotional Questionnaire

You want your questions to be carefully written so that they do not confuse the reader or suggest *correct* answers to the respondent. Here are some general guidelines:

1. Make sure your questions are clear and easily understood.
2. Keep questions short. People in a hurry won't take time to understand a long and unclear question.
3. Questions must be in sync with the purpose of the research. If the question is irrelevant to what the survey is trying to study, leave it out.
4. Don't ask questions that can be broken down into two or more questions. For example, *"Do you think the president is dishonest and a poor financial planner?"* That is really two different questions. Be wary when the word "and" appears in a question.

5. Stay away from biased words. For example, *"Do you eat a healthy breakfast or just have a Big Gulp at 7-11?"* The word "just" prejudices the answer by suggesting that the Big Gulp is less worthy than the healthy breakfast.

6. Avoid leading questions. *"Like most Washingtonians, do you drink coffee every morning?"* Watch for a hidden premise showing up in questions. Remember that the goal is to accurately determine what the respondent thinks, even if it isn't what you wish they would say. The purpose of research is to find out which of your ideas are wrong.

7. Leave out questions that require very detailed answers.

8. Avoid questions that may embarrass the respondent. Many people don't like to give their age, and most won't tell you how much money they earn. A better way is to give the respondent a broad category that they can identify with without giving away sensitive information. *"Are you between 18-24 years old, 25-49 years old? etc."* Additionally, research carries with it a certain authority that will make your ideas more persuasive to others.

Promote Your Business at Charities

Looking for a smart way to promote your entertainment business? How about a tried-and-true promotion-in method that makes you look good in the eyes of thousands of new customers and helps people in your community? Notice how many successful entertainment businesses in your town support charities. It costs less than you think to help out a non-profit group and the promotional payoff can be huge. Plus, there are lots of worthy projects in your area that could really use a helping hand. People give more to charities from November to December than any other time of year. Organizations benefiting children and the hungry get special attention from the public. However, in surveys the public always says they wished fundraisers would be held at other times of year. They are suspicious of fundraising being grouped around Christmas.

Getting the Most from Your Charity Work

Now is the time to start talking with a good non-profit organization. Contact their director and ask how your entertainment business can help. In most cases you can dedicate a small percentage of your sales to the charity. Non-profits will be ready and willing to include your name in their advertising and marketing campaigns. Have a logo, flier, short ad copy, or web site banner for them to use.

Make yourself available to join charity representatives on radio and TV talk shows and Internet chats. There are so many worthy organizations that it is often hard to choose which one to help. If you don't already have a favorite, pick one that relates to your business in some way. If you sell children's clothing, working with a charity that helps underprivileged kids at Christmas would be a good match. Some charities are better equipped to work with sponsors and the media. Others are new, have inexperienced staff, and may appreciate your business experience in showing them how to organize people and resources.

Charity Work Can Really Benefit
Your Entertainment Business! Here's How

By involving my entertainment business in Washington, DC with a non-profit Entertainment Foundation, for example the Recording Academy's programs such as MusiCare, Grammy in the Schools and The Hero Awards Ceremony, I was able to find new business prospects in need of my marketing and promotion services. I also assisted the American Women in Radio & TV with their digital photographic needs. Along with the local DC chapter's Television Emmy Awards of the Academy of Television Arts & Sciences, I was able to network fully will the larger mass media company executives and professionals.

Here's a secret. If you want to meet a celebrity entertainer up close and personal, volunteer to be a celebrity escort or program attendant at the charity event where the celebrity will be performing. (I have met and chit chatted with loads of my favorite film and TV star icons this way.) *"Ah! That's just Sonya coming to get another autograph for a friend"*, the celebrity would say. In essence, this exposure allowed me to get noticed and gained the respect of several key people in the entertainment and media industries who otherwise might not have ever known about me. They always asked me for my suggested volunteer referral. The National Association of Black Owned Broadcasters (NABOB) will only use volunteer referrals for their star-studded communication's award events.

For years, I had volunteered to serve in the communications & press offices for the local charity events along with my family and friends. The Congressional Black Caucus Foundation volunteer manager, Rhonda Bufford, could always count on my team and me. My good friend, Tonda Williams, volunteer coordinator with A Taste of DC and many, many other community & national charity events provided a regular involvement source for me. Note how many major newspapers and television stations are promoting charities this time of year. Their audience and advertisers appreciate when media works to improve the community. Try to give of your time so that your customers and prospects will feel the same way about you. As an added bonus, businesses, politicians, and community leaders are often heavily involved with charities. The people you meet can form a valuable network of contacts for your future projects and business.

Charities On The Internet

I found that BarterNet (formerly *Allbusiness.com)*, sponsored in part by American Express Financial Business services, has encouraged it's national & international on-line barter businesses to donate their *trade dollars* to an authorized and registered online charity. *Trade dollars* are what is used instead of money. This means great savings to folks like me in trying to get my family's Royal Swinton Society non-profit organization established. It has given me easy access to an international global market that might not have otherwise assisted in meeting our organization's immediate needs.

Originally, the Internet started out as a non-profit effort and still carries a strong feeling of people selflessly working to improve life. Web designer Jacky Brown recently found the Internet a perfect place to do non-profit work. *"It's turned out to be very effective. In working with Toys Not Tears, we've linked our non-profit site to the web sites of participating merchants."* Order forms can be modified so when a customer buys, a percentage of the sale is collected by the charity. It's easy and everyone involved benefits from the constant flow of customers from site to site. The group uses one site for consumers with another to recruit merchants.

Commercial Appeal and Promotion

Here is my advice to prospective sponsors of a charity event. Sometimes it's easier to get carried away trying to promote the sponsor's interests in a non-profit campaign. If it appears that sponsors are being promoted more than the work of the charity, the whole thing can backfire. Sponsors who stay discreetly in the background receive more benefit in the end. I would like to advise sponsors to focus on how they can help make things easy for clients, consumers and participants. Ease of participation is often what separates success from failure. Try to solve the problems a potential donor may have such as no time to write a check and mail it in, no extra money available, and fear their donation may not reach the right people.

Especially during the holiday seasons, lots of worthy non-profits are shouting their messages. Even though you are a sponsoring business, you may find yourself helping out on the publicity end. Use every available marketing and publicity option. It takes lots of repetition to have an impact. A well-written press release will interest editors and producers. Many e-mail newsletters are good about donating no-cost ad space for charities. Radio, TV, and newspapers will often give you free time and space if you have a cause or an event that will interest their audiences. Also think how you might be able to continue your association with a charity year after year. Those who don't notice you this year will be twice as aware the second time you participate. Many of the most successful business-charity associations have been going on for decades. There's no question your business helps others by providing valuable products, services, and ideas. You'll multiply the good feeling when you lend a hand to a non-profit charity.

Target Your Marketing for Success

At the very beginning of Community TV USA Network, we carefully planned and targeted our advertising and marketing strategies to a very narrow entertainment group at first in order to increase our odds for success and shorten the time required. My advice to you is to start by finding a solid product, service, or idea that you can sell to others. Make sure the people who would want what you sell can be found on the Internet. The on-line crowd is still just a small percentage of our total population (although that's a lot of people in total numbers). Remember that the Internet population tends to be above average in income and education.

Until recently, this population consisted of mostly young males, although the number of women and people of all ages rapidly increased last year. Try to get a merchant credit card account set-up on the Internet. Most business people use this method of payment. Can your business sell to these groups of people? Does your entertainment product or service appeal to them, or would it sell better to other groups who aren't using the Internet yet? Once you zero in on a perfect way to advertise and market your product or service to sell, consider what other products or services could be sold along with it. There's a good reason why you need to sell things that can be grouped together.

The success of your Internet business will depend almost entirely on how well you can promote it. While traditional businesses throw fortunes at radio, TV, and newspapers; the on-line entrepreneur must do most of the marketing himself or herself. Properly using newsgroups, free classified advertisements, solicited mailing lists, e-zine ads and press releases is hard enough to do with one business. You don't want to have to divide your time between two, three, or four different websites. It's much better to have one multi-faceted website for your prospects.

Work toward creating a single, recognizable Internet identity for yourself. Everyone knows *Amazon.com*. They sell books. They don't sell financial services, health items, and travel packages-just books. But *Amazon.com* sells many kinds of books and a number of different related services including an entrepreneurial opportunity. It all fits under their hotly promoted identity.

How To Promote Your Internet Entertainment Identity

Here's how to hone in on your potent Internet identity:

1. What is the main benefit that your entertainment business will offer prospects? People are only interested in the features your product or service has to offer if they can clearly see how those things benefit their company.

2. Boil your main benefit down to a short phrase you could put on a bumper sticker. My business's bumper sticker ID is *"Sonya D! Marketing Is Key-to MONEY."* Most prospects are leading very busy lives. To get their attention, you must tell them how to improve their lives quickly and in a way that's easy to understand.

3. As you promote your entertainment business services, and multiply the ways to make profits in your Internet empire, make sure that everything fits with your main bumper sticker positioning statement. One guy has a list of 70 moneymaking opportunities on his website. He has them collected under a concise promise of supplying readers with dozens of ways to make money on their own websites. It's a good way of grouping lots of different business strategies under one unified heading and *identity*. It's appealing, has lots of obvious benefits, and is easy to promote with a short bumper-sticker phrase.

4. You can't start too soon thinking about how you will market your business. When most people get an idea for a new business, they first think about how much money they'll make. The very next thought should be how they will promote the business. As you create and expand your Internet Entertainment Business Empire, keep a constant eye toward how you will market and promote it, efficiently and effectively.

Promotions for Entertainment
Corporation Agencies on the Internet

The Internet has moved to center stage for corporate advertising. Notice that major TV advertisers no longer hide their website at the bottom of the screen in tiny print. Their URL is now proudly displayed right alongside their corporate logo in the final frame. But how do you make your corporation stand out among the 200 million web sites and billions of e-mail messages that compete for attention? It can be a bewildering challenge. Call your advertising agency and they're likely to be just as confused. Here's why the Internet is such a challenge and here are some tips on how to make Internet advertising work for you. Advertisement agencies are trying to figure out how to use the Internet by the same standards they've always used in TV, radio, and newspapers. But, it isn't working. The Internet is a completely different dynamic.

Traditional media is based on a supply and demand principle that has a large number of people consuming a limited number of media outlets. That model doesn't apply to the Internet. On-line there is no shortage of programming. Everyone can be a writer, design a website, start a newsletter, or build an Internet radio station. Money doesn't necessarily enter the equation. Talent, hard work, and vision can count for everything. All this leaves the advertising business in a difficult situation.

How can they bring in revenue using their usual methods? So far, the answer has been with banners, those rectangular billboards like ads that pop up on web sites. Banners, along with targeted mailing

lists, are expected to function in the same way as print ads and com-
mercials do in traditional media. That's where the problem begins. The
Internet's huge number of websites and content providers has frac-
tionalized the audience with little agencies, like my Community TV
USA Network, well beyond anything ever known in traditional media.
The old media advertising formula simply doesn't apply to the
Internet.

For instance, in 2001 with the decline of advertising sales and with
telecommunications stock prices at an all time low, the big affiliate
commercial TV & radio stations had to fiercely compete for the billion
dollar advertisement sales. As a result, most banners and many targeted mailing lists are way over priced. Your corporation will do much
better to imitate the grass roots promotional strategies of smaller
entertainment businesses. By using these techniques on a larger level,
you can send your marketing message to millions of Internet readers
each week-without using unsolicited bulk mail.

Here's how your company can progress and grow. You will need to
place your ads into major e-zines (email newsletters). Many e-zines are
reaching subscriber levels that compete with major print publications.
You can't beat DEMC (270,000 subscribers with a clickable link to your
site) for $45 per week *www.demc.com*. I'm also impressed with the
Business Link Market Letter (600,000 subscribers for $30). You can reach
them at 319-359-9527. Hayden Mitchell has a co-op ad letter that goes
to 600,000 who have asked to be in it at about $55 per week
hayden@webthemes.com. If you want to send your articles to e-
zines…this is the place to look.

Opt-in mailing lists can be very effective if used in a highly targeted
way (which is now becoming possible). The names on these lists have
asked to be there, so you are in no danger of sending unwanted junk
mail (which, unlike regular mail, is considered a major offense by people on the Internet.). Here are some sources of opt-in targeted mailing
lists: Bonus mail: *www.bonusmail.com*. Copywriter Al Bredenberg features The Direct E-mail List Source: *www.copywriter.com-/lists*.
Bredenberg has a directory of thousands of opt-in e-mail lists. Be sure

to also check *www.PostMaster-Direct.com* (probably the best known of the bunch) *www.targ-it.com*.

Send out on-line press releases on a regular basis. Almost everyone in media has e-mail now. While each day's mountain of faxes spill out on the floor, editors and producers regard e-mail with a fresh eye. You've got material for a new press release anytime something *news-worthy* happens with your company. For example,

One day I was wondering how to contact the Royal Television Society in Scotland for the A.A. Campbell-Swinton Lectures for our USA Tartan's Day celebration. I first contacted the United States representative Roger Carter in Arizona by e-mail and he in turn referred me to Tony Currie, chairman of the Scottish Center's Royal Television Society and British Broadcasting Corporation (BBC) in Glasgow, Scotland. A couple of hours later, I had an e-mail from Scotland along with an attachment of the information that I requested. I sent the Scottish representative my online business card and a press release, all in a couple of minutes.

New services, accomplishments, and associations with people or topics in the news are always good reasons to issue a press release. A number of services will send your release via e-mail. Jennifer Howard at *asba@asba.net* will e-mail to 5,000 media outlets for $250. Also good are.*xpresspress.com* and *www.gapent.com/pr*. Then go to *www.gebbieinc.com* and browse the thousands of media contacts. It's a good idea to find several publications that specifically target your best prospects and customers. Send those editors and producers your release along with a personalized note.

Don't miss the chance to publish your own e-mail newsletter of entertainment industry news and tips. This can be one of the Internet's most powerful ways of building a strong relationship with customers and prospects. E-mail newsletters are extremely easy and inexpensive to produce. Unless you have a large budget for Internet advertising, most banner deals are not an efficient allocation of funds. It's probably just as well to go with one of the better free banner swap arrangements. For very well established banner swap services see *www.linkexchange.com* and *www.bannerswap.com*. Search engines are getting smarter, so it's more important than ever that your opening web site page contain copy that clearly targets your best customers and prospects.

Finally, don't miss out on using the free classifieds on UseNet Newsgoups that accept ads. Thousands of entertainment web surfers (who are well above average in education and income) search these newsgroups each day. There's no reason why your company shouldn't take on newsgroup marketing in a serious and consistent way. Hire two people to work three hours a day posting advertisements on Newsgroups and in website classifieds. These various Internet marketing methods are being used with great success by thousands of small businesses and entrepreneurs in the entertainment industry. Corporate marketing strategies can incorporate these same techniques on a larger scale to achieve significant results. As the Internet grows in importance to societies all over the world, your company will want to be well on its way to an established Internet presence.

Although I no longer produce the local cable TV shows because of my work in the Advertising and Marketing area, it is not surprising to me that I still receive an occasional phone call requesting that I have someone to cover their event. And I am also asked advice on how to be on their local cable TV show. This next section is dedicated to the local and upcoming entertainers. Here's to you, read on.

How to Get Your Entertainment Service, Product, Or Act On TV News—for FREE!

Few things in media are as powerful as television exposure. Anyone who has ever been on TV can tell you, a few shots on the tube and people are recognizing you in the supermarket. Local television news has taken off as one of the most trusted voices in media. Like it or not, when your local TV anchorperson says something, huge numbers of people regard it as hard truth. Imagine this scenario. You're trying hard to introduce the general public to your new entertainment service.

Advertising is expensive, so you're having to get creative to make your marketing ideas stretch. On the local nightly news, the veteran anchor-person that everyone in town has watched for 20 years turns to the camera and mentions your new service. Then he cuts to a video of a promotion at your event. Do you think this is impossible? Not at all when you know how TV news works.

You can have your entertainment business services or products featured on TV for *free* if you follow these guidelines. Always remember that Television is visual! The most important thing about television is that it is *visual*. In many cases, the story may not sound interesting or be interesting, but if it *looks* interesting, it gets on TV.

Once at a Writer's Block TV program produced by Knight Scene's productions (a TV show for authors), I positioned myself, dressed to kill, at the front of the makeshift studio's first table (Border's Bookstore in down town Washington, DC). I must add that most of the selected studio audience wore very causal street clothes for comfort on a smoldering hot summer's day. Oh, but not me!

I made dead sure that the well-known guest author and TV host would see me and allow me to ask my rehearsed question. I knew that the television viewers would also have a reasonable camera angle to see me. I intentionally didn't tell any of my co-workers that I was going to appear on the TV program. Sure enough on a Sunday morning, the first airing of the show came on and a couple of my un-expecting co-workers called me to tell me that they were shocked to see me near the stage with the well known author. They said that the television cameras immediately swung to me over and over again, regardless of me talking. While the other studio audience was speaking, the camera operators would show wide-angle views as well as close-up shots of the studio audience expressions. I got to be featured a lot. I tried not to look nervously stupid by staring into the camera so I pretended to look deeply interested in what the speakers were saying. My deep interest expressions caught the eyes of the cameramen while the rest of the audience looked somewhat bored as the questions were being delivered. Like me, everyone was really trying not to forget their rehearsed questions they were to ask the author. This is exactly how television works, so use the mass exposure to your advantage.

Contacting the Television New Department

The media is very telephone oriented. Your best bet is to call the news department and tell whomever answers all about your story. Get to the point. Make sure your story is good. Tell the reporter that answers the juicy or visual part first. Remember that while you're talking, the reporter is thinking: What's in this for us? Will our viewers be interested? Will my boss think this is a good idea? How much trouble will it be for us to get this on tape and on the air? If you can get positive answers on those three points, you've got a great shot at getting some TV exposure. Keep in mind that TV stations run short-handed and on a very tight deadline. They've got a lot of work to do in very little time.

How to Get Your Business on Television

If you can attach your product, service, or idea to a topic that the news wants to cover—you're in! Just like the person promoting an issue and who wants to get their position on the news, you can get your business on TV news by finding some way to attach your biz to a topic that TV would cover. Can your business get involved in a community service program that will be newsworthy?

Not long ago, to local two boys decided to camp out on top of their house in hopes that someone would notice them and give them tickets to a hot NBA basketball game. Their action was just goofy enough to get the TV cameras out. Everyone laughed. One sharp businessperson called a TV station and explained he was on his way over to the boys' house to offer them his tickets and bring them down off the roof. The TV news director immediately saw a story happening. He ordered a camera crew to meet the businessman as he arrived at the boys' home. Did the guy with the tickets get on TV? Yes! Did he look good to people watching? Yes! Did lots of new customers arrive at his store the next day to tell him what a great guy he was and buy a few things? Of course!

What Do Television Producers Look For?

As a former cable TV executive producer, may I suggest to you that there are several basic categories of stories that television likes to cover for it's local news segments. You won't find these written down any-where on a TV newsroom bulletin board. They are instinctive to TV assignment editors. Number one is a political story. Washington, DC is of course the place to be for politics.

Anything that has to do with local, state, or federal politics gets on TV. For instance, if the TV news producer needed information on the Tulsa, Oklahoma 1921 Race Riot Commission's work, they would call on my relative and author Mrs. Eddie Faye Gates for testimonials because she was the Chair of the Survivors Committee of the Oklahoma Commission to Study The Tulsa Race Riot of 1921. She also interviewed 167 living Black Survivors of the riot ranging in age from 78-108. Any media person who wanted to interview a riot Survivor constantly called on her (such as, 60 Minutes, Cinemax Movies, Dateline, Nightline and other major print and electronic media people from all over the world). In fact her website *www.tulsa-riot.com* got multiple hits and as a result, major national television websites linked her web page to their sites. In essence, her two books... *Miz Lucy's Cookies* and *They Came Searching* flew off bookshelves all over the U.S. and overseas.

Moreover, expect to get on TV if you mount an accepted challenge to a government official, entity, or proposal. Big community problems get the same kind of coverage. The following topics touch everyone: race relations, child abuse & neglect, local crime, garbage service, flood control, and war.

Activities that solve big community problems, or potential prob-lems, get attention too. This could be something like people planting fifty trees in the city park. Education and Health earn a lot of television coverage these days. The first one is because everyone is concerned about kids. The second is because television news viewers are dispro-portionately middle-aged. They have an increased interest in health information and issues. For instance, in 2001 a major concern was the feared health risk of Great Britain's Mad Cow disease. That may have temporarily put a damper on European travel abroad but it brought airfare prices down and made me want to take the next flight out. Heck, it was cheaper for me to fly overseas than for me to fly from one destination in the US to another US destination.

Thirdly, celebrities always get television time. The exception is if you are in the Hollywood, Los Angeles, California area. Then this will probably be close to first on the list. The reasons are clearly obvious. The man or woman who couldn't care less about the other topics mentioned will always look up when the local NBA stars or visiting movie stars come on. I will awkwardly lump sports into the entertainment category as well. Sports make up to 50% of local news in many towns.

Finally, television loves novelty. Some experts say that anything visual and original will get on. I'm not sure I agree. Strictly original stories often leave network television stations' assignment editors wondering why they should cover them. You are far better off doing something that's done once every year or two. The cameras will show up for something that they know from experience will be a winner. A Taste of DC International Food Festival in Washington, DC always has a sponsor's booth for TV affiliate NBC channel 9, and the beautifully, eye-catching International Japanese-American Cherry Blossom Festival & Parade held in the springtime almost always has all of the usual local TV and newspaper coverage.

Chapter 5

Swinton International Enterprises

An International Entertainment Virtual Office

This chapter is for the entrepreneur or non-profit organization with a new full or part-time entertainment business venture run from a small office. With a brand new start-up you will need a solution that's going to give you a professional, established image that level your competitive playing field and give customers, vendors and investors alike the confidence they need to do business with you. It's also important to have something that's flexible, something that will be able to quickly and easily adapt to your business's evolving needs and grow with you as your business grows. Agencies such as, Swinton International Enterprise is your solution! Although my agency specializes with larger entertainment clientele, we give advice at national seminars, workshops and international trade conventions.

Although, you don't need to have a website to run a successful small entertainment company, it will be to your best advantage in the long run to have a website. E-mail is the Internet's most powerful and popular feature. You don't need an office in a prestigious address. Some of the Internet's biggest earners work still in their pajamas, from a corner in their bedroom. Best of all, you don't need a wad of cash to get your small business ideas rolling. I truly feel that with hard work, dedication, vision, and a dream you are willing to see to the end are far more valuable than any lavish start-up funds. Of course, there are an endless number of ways to make money on the Internet. You can offer a service delivered conveniently by e-mail.

You can take orders for products that are shipped to customers in the United States and around the world. It's possible to start your own e-mail newsletter and get paid for running other people's ads. Building a hot website and earning money by letting companies display their banners on your pages are also options. You can also earn a good extra income simply by referring customers to other companies with a link on your website or in your e-mail messages.

Seminar and Workshop Question & Answer Sessions

Swinton International Enterprises host and participates in panel discussions around the nation and here are just a few of the insightful questions and answers we have received from our global audience by teleconferencing.

Advertising Question & Answers

Question:

I work for a local public radio station. In 2001, it got harder and harder for our business to bring in advertising revenue because of the proliferation of direct mail, AMC advertisements, 800 numbers, tele-marketers etc. What do you think will be the best and most effective way to advertise without going into so much debt? Our company does many different things for its clients.

Answer:

You might limit your advertising to the one method that brings you the most leads/customers for the money spent. Have your advertising efforts refer people to your website where they can get far more info. Also, offer an e-mail newsletter/update to send out each month. That can be a very effective and almost free way to stay in touch with customers and contacts.

Question:

Our on-line company should debut in the following few months. I believe I have targeted our initial market, an excellent way to attract them (via banner ads) and will continue to search for additional advertising avenues. Currently, I have been contacting select companies *directly* that offer banner ad space. Obviously these particular companies attract the audience in which our company is interested. Question: rather than contacting these companies *directly*, would there be any advantage to using an on-line ad agency to search out *deals* on the web, and, might an agency have savvy employees who are able to cut a more attractive deal with these companies? Please advise.

Answer:

Most online advertising agencies are going about the job pretty much the same way you are…looking for appropriate sites and trying to cut a favorable deal. They might have more expertise in negotiating. On the other hand, an agency probably wouldn't try as hard to get you a good deal as when you work the job yourself.

Question

Although we've had a web presence for over 4 years, no one but junk mailers can seem to find us! We are an international DVD recording business, with a couple years of operation, producing catalogs that go worldwide. Perhaps the problem is that we are a narrow specialty (pop, not rock), which takes some fine-tuning! Your help will be appreciated.

Answer:

Your best bet is to get Ruth Townsend's $30 membership to her huge e-zine database at *www.lifestylespub.com*. It is regularly updated with all kinds of searchable e-zine ad info.

Question:

I would like to know how to best use our radio advertising time. The local radio station uses the same two people to advertise the majority of businesses. We run the same ad every time, except for the change of new listings of homes. After listening to ads from various businesses, they all sound the same. Any ideas on how we could make ours stand out? We are the only performing arts organization that advertises our new listings as a part of our advertisement. Thank you for your time.

Answer:

Read the ad yourself. A *real* person's voice will have a bigger impact on the audience. Animate your voice more than normal. Radio listeners can't see your face, so your voice has to do double duty.

Question:

Can you tell me about the costs of commercial advertising? It seems like it would be pretty expensive, but I know a lot of small businesses are able to pull it off without blowing their budget. Do you have any tips or information about that?

Answer:

Commercial rates are all over the map. It really depends on what city you're in. I've seen TV spots for a couple of dollars in small towns on up to several thousand dollars per commercial in prime time in medium-sized to large cities. Cable TV is almost always cheaper, and you can focus on more precise audiences.

Question

We placed a 2x4 display ad in our local weekly newspaper for 13 weeks now and have received absolutely no calls. This is the busy time for our business. Would you suggest we continue and keep our name out there? Is consistency the answer? I'd appreciate any info.

Answer

You should be seeing some results by now. Try changing your ad...and also consider if the ad is reaching your best prospective customers like a trade newsletter or magazine.

Question:

I am trying to find out information about offline publications, as we are preparing to launch and advertise a new piece of film animation software from our collection.

Answer:

I've found *Wired Magazine* is a good publication to reach a great many computer and Internet professionals. We advertise in their less expensive *line ads* each month. There are a number of Mac oriented magazines on the stands these days. You might look for a new publication that has lower rates but is getting good distribution.

Question:

I am a net–worker from Greece, representing the biggest German MLM Company, which has entered the United States market on 1 Sept. 2001. My question is: how can I find and sponsor prospects in the U.S. through e-mail? Is it possible?

Answer:

Your best bet is to get a website in English, place some ads in e-zines, and write or have written for you some articles you can put in e-zines. Also, it's good to hang out in chat rooms —especially the networking discussions on AOL.

Question:

I always did okay in English classes, but I want to write up a classified advertising...and don't even know where to start. Any help would be super!

Answer:

Here are some pointers:

Write your ad in complete sentences, and then cut out the non-essential words to make it the required length. Start sentences with action words. Use short phrases. While you're at it, write several versions of your classified ad.

I usually try to knock out six at a time. Test your advertising. Run them all on free ad sites, in e-zines, newspapers, or magazines. Be sure to include a code in your response info so you will know which ad produced the inquiry or sale.

Once you find an ad that works well, leave it alone. Resist the temptation to tweak an ad that is already successful. Don't worry if you or your associates become bored with the ad. Your audience is not as close to the ad and is only assured by its repetition.

Question:

I have a question regarding Internet advertising on an individual's website. What are the average costs to charge for advertising on a small business website? How do they vary among the various types of banners and links?

Answer:

It's not unusual to charge anywhere from 25 cents to 60 cents per click-through. I've seen this figure vary widely without much justification. I would justify this rate by a site that brings in a certain type of prospects (for example, sites that pull in lots of established recording agencies can attract higher rates from advertisers).

Question:

I'm planning a big sales blitz, involving the use of sales letters. Any pointers you could give me for writing effective ones would be just great.

Answer:

Here's a very simple idea that works wonders for any kind of writing: Keep your paragraphs short. Sales copy should rarely use paragraphs longer than three sentences. One and two sentence paragraphs work great. Why? Most readers are in a big hurry. Long paragraphs look intimidating and hard to read. Short chunks of copy separated by white space immediately say, *"Get this information fast."* You can use the short paragraphs strategy for web copy, sales letters, and e-mail messages, too.

Question:

My brother and I sell our CDs and we have worn ourselves out in the past year trying to get some kind of word out there to help us increase sales. We are about ready to quit and go back to our day jobs. It feels like we've done everything.

Answer:

Occasionally I will meet a businessperson who has done a lot of advertising but still isn't selling much. It isn't that they haven't tried. The list of advertising they attempted can be staggering. Here are some common reasons that even well promoted products don't sell: Your advertising isn't targeted to the right market. This is probably the most common problem.

A company advertises with a media that reaches a mass audience (like TV or daily newspapers) but reaches too few of their customers who belong to a *specific* group. Secondly, there may not be any real market for the product. It may seem like a great idea, but nobody wants it—at least, not yet. Thirdly, customers may feel that your business is too small to sell the product. One man knew his medium-sized business could supply the needs of major customers, but they didn't buy until his company grew into a big corporation. *"We could have served them just as well before, but they wouldn't buy because they thought we weren't big enough."* Sometimes tightly targeted media does not always reach the audience it claims to reach, and therefore you must try running a test first to see if you get results before spending big bucks.

Question:

What is the best way to advertise on Billboards? Should I use my logo, pictures or should I use text only!

Answer:

Your best bet is to have a picture that helps tell your story … accompanied by a very few words. Of course, your logo should be there as well. The key is to get attention, make a simple point, and do it all while someone is driving by at high speed. A picture that tells the story is the most important part.

Question:

How can I make my yellow pages ad stand out from my competitor's? What the sales rep showed me looked like all the other bands' advertisements, but for $3500 a year I want something that stands out. How can I get my money's worth?

Answer:

Gina Davis, our editor, is also a design expert. Here's her answer: "*If a sales rep is offering you a boring set of clip art and typefaces, ask if you can substitute your own. I just opened the yellow pages under band-music," and immediately noticed an ad using 3-D graphics*". Not only does it draw my eye from all the other ads, but also it continues to draw my eye. It practically pops out of the pages—definitely a way to catch a customer's eye. You can also try the unorthodox approach. Look through clip art collections for a cartoon character holding a paint palette, or another image associated with colors or paint. You can find tons of free clipart (look at the disclaimer to be sure it's copyright free!) on sites like *www.clipart.com*. Use an image that is simple and clearly drawn—think about how it will look when it is reproduced in the phone book. Finally, you might consider putting a photo of your band in the ad. It will give your audience the feeling that they already know you.

Question:

What should I charge for my e-book and for ads in it?

Answer:

So many people are giving them away for free that it's getting hard to charge a lot for e-books. Some are selling for $5. $12.95 is a good price point. I've heard from some that they can't sell an e-book at $19. As for ad prices, it would depend on how many people you can get to download your e-book. $10 per 1,000 is the usual rate for e-zines.

Question:

I am a second year International Business student at the University of Maryland, College Park. We are working on a paper on advertising repetition. Why is repetition important?

Answer:

The idea behind repetition is that people are so busy and see so many advertising messages during each day that an ad has to be repeated over and over before people will pay attention and act on it.

Question:

We are a small company involved in film animation and our core audience is basically children-preschool to elementary. Do you have an affordable way for us to get to them?

Answer:

Your best bet would be to advertise in preschool and early childhood publications. The people who mostly read these magazines are school administrators, teachers, day care providers and parents. Beyond that, you could use the classic sales letters followed by phone calls to area early learning centers.

Question:

I decided to start out a newspaper that is community centered, and particularly focused on kids. How do I get advertising for the first issue?

Answer:

In order for you to get a community newspaper started, you will need to assure that a certain number of copies will be delivered free…just so that you can guarantee a level of readership. Then you will need to sell advertising based on those numbers. Contact advertisement agencies in your area to see if any are interested.

Question:

Why are some TV commercials so obnoxious?

Answer:

Good point! The theory in advertising is that more obnoxious commercials appeal to teens and 20ish men. The other reason is advertising folks have industry fads that don't make much sense to people outside their industry. I have a feeling this is one of their fads.

Question:

Could you give any advice for a small start-up business with limited resources? It is a dance studio.

Answer:

If most of your customers are coming from homes in nearby neighborhoods, you might try putting flyers on doors. Some towns are more open to this than others…but it works extremely well and is the lowest cost advertising around. Staple a rubber band to the flyer and loop it around doorknobs. Include a headline a photo of somebody in a dramatic pose. Include your web address so people can check it out for more info.

Question:

I have a client who has a radio program he would like to have syndicated. The show is good, the market is right, the timing terrific. However, I do not have the contacts.

Answer:

Check out the resources linked at *www.rronline.com.* It is the home page of Radio and Records, the industry's main trade publication. In most cases you will find a syndication form. Call or e-mail to find the right person, and send your tape.

Question:

We design and host websites and would rather outsource our work to the printing and advertising industries that have a built-in client base rather than going directly after the end users one by one.

Answer:

Good idea! See about doing a co-op deal with them. Maybe supply some free service to their customers (like one free web page). Radio and newspapers are starting to give customers a web site, and then include the URL in the customers advertising. Advertising media is always looking for things to add to their packages.

Marketing—Questions & Answers

I am interested in marketing my services on the Internet. I have the time and expertise to start a service-based consulting business. I have reserved a website but obviously have not developed it much. I am near Columbia, South Carolina and I attend networking events sponsored by many professional organizations in my field of work. In particularly, I am looking for interesting business to business offers. There are a few clients that I am interested in, however. Do you have any marketing recommendations for me?

Answer:

Congratulations, you're probably miles ahead of your competition. Market and promote your service by using the search engines MEG Tags. This should greatly interest a large segment of people who need your particular service. It's also important to pick parts of your service that you would like to highlight.

Question:

I'm a novice at this e-mailing business. Your advice in the last workshop sponsored by Swinton International Enterprises on marketing was very beneficial to say the least. In a short, while I plan on using your services to market a product I have, right now I'm interested in learning of a reputable bulk e-mailer you would feel comfortable in recommending to me.

Answer:

There are two kinds of bulk mail: opt-in and unsolicited (commonly called SPAM). Unsolicited mail is cheap to send, but it rarely works. Most servers are now set up to filter it out so their members don't get it. You'll also get a heap of grief from people who don't want spam, and your website and ISP can get shut down. Opt-in bulk mail, where people have asked to be on a list, can work well, but it's a lot more expensive (20 cents per name is not unusual). See *www.postmasterdirect.com* and *www.yesmail.com*. I find that advertising in e-zines, either with a classified or a solo advertisement is a far more affordable way to do opt-in mailing.

Question:

We'd like to ask you about your marketing. *'How do we rent a mailing list of Canadian businesses."* We're from Canada, so where do we locate companies that we can rent a list from that serves the Canadian Region?

Answer:

Your best bet is to check the Standard Rate and Data Service directory of mailing lists. See their site at *www.srds.com*. Also check local phone books for *mailing list brokers* and *direct mail*.

Question:

I'm a Marketing Manager for a small film studio company. I have a Sales Manager that would like a marketing report done in a basic form and in a detailed form. Do you have any examples I can use? He's been unhappy with every approach I have used so far. Any ideas?

Answer:

Marketing reports can take just about any kind of form…from a few paragraphs to dozens of pages. Generally you look at your target customer, figure out what media can reach them, then buy as much as your budget will allow. Test along the way to see what is working.

Throw out what doesn't work and do more of what does work. All marketing plans follow that line of thinking to one degree or another.

Question:

I have read some very impressive research on e-mail marketing strategies. My question is simply, how often should users receive e-mail? I work for a commercial, content-driven website with a sub-scriber base of 200,000+. Some people want to issue a bi-weekly e-mail, one short and to the point, and some people would like a content-based lengthy e-mail. Others want to have a short e-mail per week. Is there a better strategy here? Any advice you may have would be greatly appreciated.

Answer:

We have two e-mail newsletters...one that comes out once each week and another that is daily. We see lots of crossover, but it is very hard to get a daily newsletter subscriber list over about 7,000. Some people who send info-packed ezines out every two weeks or even just once a month get excellent response. I'd say once per week is about right.

Question:

I want your suggestions on promoting our products directly to the consumer through limited advertising and other ground activities throughout the big cities. The general profit margin is around 20-25%. Kindly tell me how much we should spend as a marketing budget in percentage of expected sales or profit? Is there a general rule about that?

Answer:

Most experts feel it is good to spend 20% of your budget on market-ing and advertising. Of course, this varies greatly from one business to the next. A new business trying to get started in a very competitive entertainment industry might have to spend 80% while an established business with lots of return customers might spend as little as 2% on staying in touch with their customer list.

Question:

I've noticed that some website referrals have a much lower click through-to-sale ratio than referrals from websites that are closely related to the product a company sells. How would you suggest that affiliate marketing be mixed in?

Answer:

You could have your own affiliate program (*affiliateshop.com* has a good low-cost system) and insist that affiliates have sites that cover a topic similar to yours. Several successful online entertainment compa-nies have done this. You can also only join affiliate programs that closely compliment your entertainment website's topic. Search through the vast and always updated directory at *www.associatepro-grams.com*.

Question:

What is your absolute favorite book on Internet marketing and search engine ranking?

Answer:

I have found that the best thing on search engine ranking is the free report (more like a short book) at *WebMarketingNow.com* Jerry West stays on top this constantly changing field. The best book in general on

Internet marketing is Jim Daniels' Insider Internet Marketing (*www.bizweb2000.com*). Jim says more in fewer words than anybody. There are a number of good books on *Amazon.com* Search for *"internet marketing"*; then look for titles under the *"people who bought this book also bought"*…

Question:

With the explosion of information and the new sophisticated buyer, is complete frankness better or do I still need to use some sales techniques? How do you sell to a friend? How do you sell yourself best to an employer? How do you market yourself in a way to customers on the Internet so they would read the e-mail and not consider it junk?

Answer:

Very good questions! I think you have to get to know your prospect, then offer them something they value. People will always pay attention to a benefit that speaks directly to their most pressing problems.

Question:

A radio show wants to interview me about my booklet. Should I give away all the info that is in the booklet, or hold back in the interview?

Answer:

I've found that giving away all the info in an interview is good. In the end, the show won't be able to provide nearly all the info that's in your booklet. Most listeners are doing other things while they listen and miss half of what you say. Those are the folks that will buy the booklet to make sure they get all your information.

Question:

I'm looking for low-cost ways to market my small business. I've thought of flyers in areas where there are homes that would suit my painting, and a magnetic sign for the side of my car.

Answer:

Both are very good, effective ways to market at low cost. I'm a big fan of fliers. Staple a rubber band to the flyer and wrap it around doorknobs.

Promotions—Questions & Answers

Question:

When a company gives some free offer in an attempt to improve its reputation, might it also decrease the company's reputation, making them seem less reliable or lower class?

Answer:

In most cases, offering something free works very well to increase business, awareness, and reputation. In some businesses the word *free* seems less dignified, so they say *complimentary,* or *no cost.* Of course, those are just fancy ways of saying *free,* but they do sound a bit more professional.

Question:

If I want to capitalize on the "New Year's Resolution" syndrome to launch my opportunity seeker business, do you think I should get it out there shortly after January 1 or slightly before?

Answer:

You would probably be safe to start ASAP. You might be able to cash in on the November run... then still be fresh for January. It will take that long to get on search engines.

Question:

I am the owner of a motivational speaker website. We are attempting to capture a large portion of this market, and we have a pretty nice website dedicated to that end. I would like you to look at our site and give us your feedback on what you think we may be doing incorrectly at present. We get a fair amount of hits a day, but sales are slumping.

Answer:

Your site's design is outstanding and very professional. You might add a paragraph or so of copy near the top of the opening page that explains what your site is all about. Many people look for this right at the beginning, before clicking further into the site. That is a very good idea putting photos on the opening page. People feel like they know you, and this creates deeper trust right away.

Question:

We would like you to take a look at our website and give us any recommendations that you can. We are interested in purchasing a web copy rewrite package in the future.

Answer:

Your site looks very good. I think you could include some testimonials from others (customers, experts, and etc.). Perhaps you should put a few of the most important sentences in bold or red, or set them apart from the rest of the text in some way. The idea on this last point is to allow busy people to quickly skim the copy and get the idea before deciding the read the whole thing. Many simply won't read it if it looks like there's too much copy. Others won't buy unless there is a lot of copy. This method lets you appeal to both.

Question:

I have my own talent agency. I just purchased the business in February, and I really need to get my name out there so people know it. The business has been in town for 5 years, but people still tell me they have never heard of it. I want everyone to know my company's name, just like the major agencies. I'm just starting out, so I need something that is low cost to get the business going.

Answer:

One way to get known quickly would be for you or someone on your team to appear on local talk radio programs. Offer information on how people can model part-time or full-time. Most TV stations have an entertainment coordinator/editor that would welcome you if you have good info to offer.

Question:

Could you elaborate on the process of how to send an Internet press release? How long before we may see results? What circuits will the release go to, and what percentage of media sources will actually use the release? What clipping services or alternatives/-suggestions can we use to track results?

Answer:

More than half of media lists are radio (due their very large numbers in the US). Radio tends to use a release right away, although it can take several days. TV works much the same way. Newspapers can take anywhere from a few days to a few weeks, and magazines generally take one to two months. There is no accurate way to predict response, and it is often difficult to measure response without using an expensive clipping service (and even that wouldn't allow you to see what is happening with broadcast media). In general, a release does better if it relates to a larger topic that the media is already covering.

Your best bet is to watch for sudden increases in hits to the site, or for more calls. Editors used to call the company for more details, but that doesn't happen as often now. Be sure to place your release on the website and register the page with major search engines (alta vista, excite, and hot bot reach about 85% of users).

Question

What is the average amount of traffic an Internet press release will be able to draw?

Answer:

As you can imagine, press release results can vary widely. Better stories, more interesting announcements, or helpful advice tend to get used more often by media. One client says he always gets 1,000 hits to his website when a release goes out. Others report that getting on CNN, Oprah, in major magazines, etc. is effective. One way to increase results is to send your release yourself along with a short personal note to local media. Another is to put your release up on your website and register the page with search engines (lots of reporters surf the internet for stories).

Question:

I know that direct mail works for traditional businesses. However, will it work for my website as well?

Answer:

There are an increasing number of Internet businesses that are turning to traditional sales letters sent through the mail. It's a tried-and-true method that brings results. You can mail your web site announcement, new product release, or price specials to as many people as you want without being accused of spamming. Check the catalog of mailing lists available from *www.SRDS.com.* It's a standard in the Direct Mail industry. Look for fresh lists that are tightly targeted to your best customers. Direct Mail response rates can be quite low. Get more leads by sending people to your website to collect a free offer.

Question:

I am an entertainment web designer who is doing some online marketing. I am curious about 'electronic press kits.' I've heard the term but have no idea what one would look like—so I have no clue on how to put one together! Any ideas?

Answer:

Electronic press kits are a great way to generate free media publicity. There is no firm rule on what needs to be included in a press kit (hard copy or electronic) but you will look like a pro if you include this information:

1. Company background. This gives the reporter a good idea of what your company does, who is in charge, and what you sell. Tell how your company started and list important customers.

2. A press release. This is a single sheet that announces newsworthy information. It can be a new product announcement or info the media audience will find interesting.

3. Traditional press kits often include a question and answer sheet. This can be translated online into a FAQ (frequently asked questions) page. Think of questions the press might ask (or you would like them to ask). You will be surprised at how often media folks will follow your Q&A during an interview.

4. Add a graphic or two to fill out your package.

5. Be sure to include telephone numbers and e-mail addresses where you can be contacted at all times.

Question:

I would like to know what company could provide me targeted E-mail lists?

Answer:

You can find good opt-in e-mail lists at *bulletmail.com, targ–it.com,* and *postmasterdirect.com.* Unsolicited bulk mail lists get terrible response and bulk is now illegal in several states with North Carolina ready to prosecute outside their own state line).

Chapter 6

Who Wants to be a Billionaire?

The Secret Weapon of the Entertainment Industry:
Introducing the Billion Dollar Barter Game

Regis Philbin had the right idea for his popular ABC game show, *"Who Wants to be a Millionaire?"* but allow me to introduce you to an even more grandiose idea. The billion dollar barter industry is the media conglomerates most coveted *secret weapon*. Media moguls have been using this top-secret weapon of financial leverage for many years. I personally have enjoyed using this type of financial leverage for my clients at Community TV USA Network and also for Swinton International Enterprises. The idea of bartering dates back to prehistoric time and was the most common way of exchanging goods and services for a fee before the invention of coins and paper money. Bartering is an old fashioned way of adequately exchanging what you have for what you want or vice versa.

Why should entertainment companies, large and small, need to use bartering as a viable means of doing business? Entertainment executives know that because of the magnitude of benefits that successful advertising and marketing representatives, media buyers and promotion executives enhance their delivery, bartering is an essential way of profiting with low cash output.

In other words, bartering increases buying power, conserves cash flow, and effectively moves surplus inventory. Small agencies such as Community TV USA Network utilize a combination of cash, barter, promotions and other creative media buying strategies to lower their clients' costs. This helps to guarantee more media avenues for their money. In the United States and overseas, professional teams of bartering specialists help to assure that the international and national broadcast market, radio station management, media buyers and media placement representatives are delivered with optimum efficiency and effectiveness.

The Department of Commerce says that barter in its various forms, accounts for about 30 % of the world's total business. Currently, over 250,000 United States businesses actively use organized barter. The International Reciprocal Trade Association (IRTA) recently announced that U.S. barter transacted through commercial barter brokers exceeds eight billion dollars annually and the Internet will only proliferate this exchange even more.

Here Comes Business...Can you handle it?

Jeremy Alexander says, *"Sonya gives you efficient ways to manage lots of customer questions, orders, and e-mail in her workshop called HERE COMES BUSINESS. Can you handle it?"* Although the workshop is tailored to the entertainment industry, just about anyone who owns a website can learn from the information. Included is also a list of places to get *free* promotional tools! Once your on-line entertainment business starts getting attention and pulling in sales and work orders, your workload will increase. Customers will ask questions, orders will fly in, and e-mail will invariably start to stack up. Much of running a successful Internet business has to do with knowing how to use e-mail well.

Remember to use a signature (sig) file on all of your e-mail messages. Thirty million people use e-mail every day, so it makes sense to pack your messages with a special dose of promotion. A sig file is your business name, a brief line about what you do and what benefit you bring to customers, your website address, and your contact info. A sig file can be a good and acceptable source of advertising when posting to otherwise noncommercial Use Internet newsgroups. Find a newsgroup that discusses your area of expertise and post a message offering useful information. Your sig file can direct people back to you and your website for additional help. Handling the rush of response. Now that you have done all this promotion, don't be surprised if you wake up to find your e-mail box brimming with questions and orders from dozens or hundreds of customers. You will need an informed and organized way of smartly working leads and sales.

Follow-up is key to selling. Some customers need seven to 10 contacts with you before they buy. This can increase sales 50%. If you are busy answering e-mail from a flood of new customers, it can be hard to find the time or remember to keep up with those you have already made contact with. Fortunately, e-mail offers a nearly free way to repeatedly follow-up with interested prospects. Let your auto responders do the work for you. These simple online gizmos send your sales information to anyone who sends an email to your auto responder address. The auto responder then sends your customer additional messages and reminders at intervals, which you determine.

A prospect could get your free report on day one, your sales letter on day two, and your special price list on day three. A week later your auto responder could send them a reminder with another message set to go out next month. All this is done automatically without you ever having to lift a finger. E-mail programs like Eudora and Pegasus let you quickly route messages into files on your computer. You can also set up templates with answers to questions you get all the time. Instead of typing the same answer to a question over and over, you can click a button and the answer appears. This saves you many hours otherwise spent doing e-mail chores.

Few if any ideas work perfectly the first time. Look at any failures as learning experiences and as steps you take toward success. Test your products, services, and marketing. Analyze the results, make adjustments, and try again. You can track the effectiveness of advertising by directing respondents to a special email address or web page. For example, have them reply to *info12@yoursite.com* or *www.yoursite.com/info12* ("info12" could be your code for the ad you placed in a specific e-zine).

The Internet is so hot and so unstoppable that leaders in Washington, D.C. actually have to take steps to slow down the economy. The Internet is not only changing the way we do business, it is also changing the way people live their lives all over the world. Most importantly, the Internet levels the playing field. You no longer have to get a major bank loan or sell millions in stock to build your home-based business empire. Anyone working from home can have a part-time or full-time business earning a steady income on the Internet. Even if your small entertainment business is already working well on the Internet, look for ways you can extend your online activities to this global networking community. In the near future, all businesses could be online. Make your move *now* to stake your claim on the bustling Internet frontier.

You can get just about anything you need to run your home-based Internet business without paying a cent. Most of the promotional and administration tools mentioned in this book are offered online at no charge. Get a free website space at www.*tripod.com*, *www.homestead.com* and *www.xoom.com*. These services also include easy programs to help you build your web-site, even if you do not have experience. The web-site of *www-.sendfree.com* offers up to 20 *free* auto responders and runs your ad at no charge on their big auto responder network. Get *free* auto responders that automatically send up to 10 return messages at: *www.fastfacts.net*, *www.zinfo.net*, and *www.smartbotpro.net*. Register your website with over 400 search engines free at *www.submit4free.com*.

I get a big chuckle out of experts who preach the joys of working from home. When I had my Children's Cable TV Workshop Performing

Arts classes, I used the extra room in my condo as a training studio for kindergartner and preschoolers. As a professional trainer, I had the older kids come after school to take acting, modeling or dancing lessons from me. Although my arrangement was convenient for me, the kids' noise and energy created wear and tear on my psyche.

To the kids' parents, I may have made things look easy, but in reality that was far from the truth. Experts advise that this isn't the way a successful work-at-home business is supposed to operate. The professional home-worker is told to make clients think he or she is in a big, plush office in a mirror-covered professional building. *"Never allow noise from kids and pets to be heard and never answer the phone 'hello.' Clients won't take you seriously,"* they write.

Let's be realistic for a second. Of the six million North Americans who work from their houses, I'll bet more than half have noisy kids, dogs, and unfolded laundry competing for their attention. Yet, studies routinely show work-at-homers often get as much or more done than those in the office. Here are a few ideas to help you succeed with a home business when you have lots of family responsibilities to deal with at the same time:

Don't worry about kids interrupting a phone call. Being there for family is cool these days. The vast majority of business people wish they were at home with their kids. More often than not, when a small voice starts demanding a popsicle in the middle of an important negotiation, the client on the other end will be delighted. *"Are you working at home? How neat! Isn't it wonderful that you can be there for your kids,"* your client will say.

Working non-stop with full concentration is only for people locked in a corporate office. Get used to working in a start-and-stop fashion. When you see your work is about to be interrupted, don't stop at a natural place. Stop in the middle. It will help you get restarted when time allows.

The feeling you must be constantly productive at all times is a recent invention of our industrial societies. The majority of the world's people are much more laid back. Take a little more time to get a project finished. Oddly, your productivity will increase.

If you are a firm of one, promote your oneness to the world. Every customer wants to feel like he or she can talk to the person in charge. That's never a problem for people who do business with you. Think of all the big corporations that strive to be identified with their founder. Microsoft has Bill Gates, KFC has the Colonel, and Wendy's has Dave. They spend millions to ensure you identify their mammoth corporation with a single individual in charge.

Get over the idea that TV is bad for kids. It is a popular, healthy, worthwhile activity when used wisely in moderate doses. People who sell books perpetrate most of TV's criticism. There is a lot of terrifically educational TV programs and videos that kid love to watch. Plan to get a project underway while the kids (we'll include spouses, too) engage in some quality TV consumption.

A few hundred years ago people always worked with their kids under foot. It was only when business became dominated by factories that workers were forced to leave their children at home (and even then, it took at least 100 years to make workers change). You certainly can be a success working at home while taking care of children—even if your children are rowdy, noisy, and demanding.

When I had the Children's Cable TV Workshop in my condo studio, I earned a good living working at home and so can you! Luckily the parents didn't expect me to always pick up the phone when they called. It's not that I didn't want to talk with them, but probably that my preschoolers had just swiped my keys and were heading for the parking lot or the swimming pool.

How To Successfully Barter for Your Advertising, Marketing and Promotion Needs

Nothing is more powerful on the World Wide Web than people agreeing to barter each other's advertisements. Ad exchange networks were one of the first things to appear on the Internet. Get someone else to display your advertisement on their website and you have just doubled the number of people who know about you. You can explode the number of prospective customers by getting your ad on a big group of websites. That's the idea behind barter popular banner exchanges and one new service that is bringing the advertising exchange concept to e-mail. Now you don't even need a web site to take advantage of an advertising exchange program. *Link-Exchange.com* was one of the first free ad exchange networks and now has over 400,000 participating web sites. Microsoft recently took over the network dedicating lots of cash to making ad exchanges bigger than ever. Here's why.

Successful Entertainment Internet Business

The Internet is a great equalizer giving opportunity to anyone willing to roll up his or her sleeves and go to work. But how do you build your own online empire when you're already busy with job and family? Here are several tried-and-true shortcuts to get your online business up and profitable in record time. Those snazzy corporate websites now cost one million dollars and more. Customers expect your site to look almost as good. Professional designers spend years and thousands of dollars purchasing the right programs and learning how to use them. You can skip the learning curve by using a good template-based web design system. *JustWebIt.com* and others offer free systems you can use online to build your site. Simply type your headlines into the supplied boxes, add your copy, pull up the right graphics, and list your product prices. For a more advanced look that makes you look like you spent thousands on designers, try NetStudio. Get the free download at *NetStudio.com*.

Skip the shopping cart and go with a good third-party credit card processor or one of the new generations of all-in-one solutions. A number of firms like paypal.com and ccnow.com give you an online order form, process your customer's credit cards, and deposit the funds into your bank account. They charge healthy percentages, but it's a no-cost way to start taking cards.

Goemerchant.com has a one-click "buy-me" system that lets you easily link their shopping cart to any product or service on your site. Watch for hidden merchant account fees. Especially be wary of credit card companies that say your shopping cart can be tied into their system with simple programming.

Buying visitors for your website can be very expensive. Advertising and marketing costs mount quickly. You can get thousands of visitors free by building attractive features into your site. You can offer your clients free articles for their pressing needs. You can also make your site attractive to search engines. Keep your site's theme narrow and well focused. When prospects type a word that describes you into a search engine, your site will be far more likely to come up if your copy revolves around that search topic.

Offer a service with plenty of profit built in. Think of something you, or someone you hire, can do to help businesses. The lion's share of commerce on the Internet consists of products and services sold to businesses. A good service can cost you very little to deliver and it can command a high price. Create your own in-house email list. Spam is ineffective and often illegal. It's a much better idea to offer a newsletter or monthly update packed with helpful information your customers will appreciate. They will respond by saving your e-mail, printing it off, and forwarding it to associates. Cut the time of producing and sending your newsletter with the no-cost Ezine Builder at *e-zinez.com*. Onelist.com and *Topica.com* offer free list management services that can save you hours each week. Get help writing your website copy. Effective copy can make a huge difference in how many people buy from your website.

If having a professional writer sounds too expensive, then you should write your copy yourself and have a professional writer edit for you. It may take no more than an hour of the professional's time. Become an expert on something. Experts are in constant demand. Everyone wants to buy from an expert. Becoming known, as an authority is probably easier than you realize. Spend time at your local library reading up on a subject your customers care about. Use search engines to find more information online. Jot down the things you learn and write them into short articles. Use your own words. These eight simple shortcuts are the mortar behind many successful Internet businesses. Use them to smartly cut costs and speed your path to success.

Strong Internet Business

Day after day news media warns us the world's economy may be in serious trouble. Storm clouds are on our economic horizon. Japan, once the most profitable nation in the world, is having deep money troubles. Experts say Japan is now where the United States was at the start of our Great Depression back in the 1930s. Russia, Latin America, and Southeast Asia are also having serious economic problems. Who knows, a world depression could be on the way. Does this gloom and doom apply to the Internet? Will thousands of small Internet entertainment business be forced to close down? I don't think so. Here's why.

Internet business is still brand new. Even the old-timers have only been on-line for three or four years. In many ways, we're just now figuring out how Internet business works. And guess what? It appears to be very different from regular business. Small and versatile is a big advantage. Big businesses dominate the traditional business world. The Walt Disney & Discovery Channels have successfully competed with the larger affiliate television stations. Three out of four Internet businesses are very small, often only one person working from home.

A single person still working a regular job runs some of the most successful web sites. They take care of their on-line business before work, during lunch, and late into the evening. Small businesses are very versatile. They can change directions at a moment's notice. That's a big advantage when times are hard. Consider the large job layoffs of the Bush Administration in 2001.

A big company has specialized employees and materials stockpiled to fill a particular need. If the economy changes and that need dries up, the big biz is stuck. Meanwhile, the one person Internet entertainment business can change its direction in an afternoon. You can take down your big website offering music CDs and put up an equally impressive website showing people how to play a piano. No employees to retrain. No leases to get out of.

The wonderful thing about the power of the Internet is its ability to personalize. Every indicator of how the future will be points to a much greater demand for personalized services. Instead of buying a one-size-fits-all service from suppliers, you will enjoy services and products that are closely tailored to exactly what you want and need. Internet leaders, including Bill Gates, have said they believe the future of the Internet lies in personalized services supplied by small companies and individuals. The Internet may be at odds with the current market. This idea is a tad complicated, but I think it's important to understand why the Internet probably won't feel the pinch of a bad economy. Market economics, the basic principles that govern business, doesn't seem to fit the Internet. Market economics generally encourage big companies to get bigger and they end up, buying up and out-maneuvering smaller companies.

The biggest companies dominate their industry. Sometimes they grab a huge percentage of all sales in their particular field. This is very hard to do on the Internet. It may be impossible to build an Internet-based monopoly. I may raise millions of dollars and create the biggest, coolest website business in history. That doesn't keep you and 1,000 other aggressive folks from doing the same thing tomorrow and taking my advantage away.

Here is what can you do to profit from coming hard times? Economic downturns can be scary times. It's hard to know if you should start or expand a business or keep your money in the bank. Don't spend money you don't have to. Yet economic hard times can pose a terrific opportunity for people working in a new area like the Internet. While traditional business models stall, Internet business surges ahead on the shoulders of people using very different ways of doing business. Make your Internet presence big. Expand your website. Jazz up the look. Add lots of helpful articles, add links to useful sites, and create alliances with other entrepreneurs. Keep your website as focused as you can. Let people know you specialize in an area or line of products. When customers need a particular thing, they'll know you're the specialist that can give them personalized help.

Finally, remember the wise old saying: When business is bad, advertise. The Internet shows little honor to those who come in with lots of start-up money. Instead, the Internet rewards those who are popular. The more visitors your website and e-mail box have, the more power you have on the Internet. Publicize your website, your business, and your name. Distill your name and main benefits down to a short, easy sentence and put that sentence everywhere you can without spamming. Advertise in e-mail newsletters. Put banners ads on sites like your own. Send out press releases to media. Participate in newsgroups. Paint your promotional efforts with big broad strokes. Spend as much as half your time promoting. By looking big and providing tightly focused products and services to a well-defined group of customers, you can ride the Internet wave into the future. It may well be a future that gives the Internet new and greater prominence.

Barter for Your Advertisement and Marketing Campaign

Advertising and marketing are the best ways to use bartering to attract cash business. Advertising media, including radio, television, magazines and newspapers are all available on trade. After all, there is not a way to store advertising media and sell it later, so media companies welcome trade. If a minute in precious advertising time passes at a local radio or television station without an advertiser buying it, that minute is lost forever. The same is true in various ways for all other advertising media.

The good news is that bartered advertising and marketing, as well as promotions, are very affordable to small businesses. Because employee benefits represent a major cash cost for large businesses and are rapidly becoming unaffordable for many small businesses, bartering can represent an opportunity to cut cost and generate cash income for the individual entrepreneur. Take for instance my dentist friend in Gulfport, Mississippi. If he used bartering as a means of regularly doing business, he could take patients and use a virtual insurance company to bill his clients' company for reimbursement in cash. Businesses such as hotels, mortgage, insurance and utility firms often use bartering for their commercial customers. Barter still often plays an important role in international trade with countries whose currencies are not readily convertible as in the case of Germany.

Bartering in the Entertainment World of Film

The World Wide Web has leveled the playing field for small entertainment companies, such as independent film producers, for their piece of the million-dollar market in film productions and services. In 2001, a seasoned senior interactive marketing director based in Hollywood, California realized that the staggering billion dollar bartering system was alive and kicking in the movie industry. He commented *"As an interactive account representative working with both feature film studio executives and their advertisement agencies, I have bartered services in order to trade access to their celebrity stars via interviews and "not-yet-released" film soundtracks for advertisement space on entertain-mint websites"*. He also added *that before an account representative approach a movie studio or advertisement agency with an interactive marketing and promotion plan, they must first find out the company's projected budget, including actual dollars being spent on the more traditional media of magazines, newspaper, radio and television"*.

As you can see by now that bartering advertising, marketing and promoting is a standard practices throughout the world of entertainment and media. By utilizing the top-secret billion dollar bartering system of the mega-media conglomerates, you too can enhance the cash flow of your small entertainment business. Individuals are no longer limited in promoting their services. Even on a shoestring budget you can maximize your profits and cash flow potential. In essence, bartering just may be the method your business can use to catapult you into an Internet celebrity with star power success.

I truly hope that this resource book of advertising, marketing and promoting on the Internet has helped you overcome the mass confusion of using the Internet to your advantage. I look forward to hearing from you in the future and who knows, STAR POWER: Internet Celebrity may be the only ticket you will ever needed to gain insight for your financial success.

If this book has assisted you in anyway, please let us know by contacting us on *success-story@internet-celebrity.com*. And remember, STAR POWER: Internet Celebrity

"Where fame and stardom is Only a galaxy away
And in your case, a click of a mouse"!

About the Author

Sonya D. Swinton is a multi-talented Internet pioneer. She specializes in advertising, marketing and promotions for the entertainment industries of fashion, film, television, musical recordings and professional sports. As a twelve-year veteran in mass media advertising, marketing and promotions, Ms. Swinton is also an award-winning photographer. She is an international consultant and motivational speaker for the phenomenal power of the Internet.

She has an advanced Graduate Certificate from Howard University, Washington, DC. a Masters Degree in Education from the Pennsylvania State University and a Bachelor of Science degree from the University of Arkansas at Pine Bluff. Most of all, she is noted for her charisma and flare for the creative visual designs of several interactive websites.

Bibliography

Bacon, Mark S. *Do-It-Yourself Direct Marketing Secrets for Small Business.*
John Wiley & Sons (1997)

Betancourt, Marian. *The Best Internet Businesses You Can Start.* Adams
Media Corporation, Holbrook, MA, (1999).

Camarda, Bill. *Cheapskate's Guide to Bargain Computing.*
Prentice Press. (1997)

Daniels, Jim. Insider's Guide to Internet Marketing *(1998)*

Fraser, George. Success Runs In Our Race *(1994)*

Gates, Eddie Faye. *Miz Lucy's Cookies.* Coman & Associates. (1996)

Gates, Eddie Faye. *They Came Searching: How Blacks Sought the Promised
Land In Tulsa.* Eakin Press (1997)

Levinson, Jay Conrad. *Guerrilla Advertising.* Houghton & Mufflin.
(1998)

Philips, Michael and Rasberry, Salli. *Marketing Without Advertising.*
Nolo Press. (2001)

Schmeiser, Lisa. *Web Design Template Sourcebook.* (1999)

Stanek, William R. *Increase Your Web Traffic in a Weekend.* (2000)

Index

0-595-22164-5